Govern of Rhode [...] a debt default [...] shutdown could render the President a ceremonial position with no capacity to intervene in a secession after the next election. A government is primarily a legal and financial organism. If there is going to be a response, it will have to be coordinated on the local or state level by the Emergency preparation agencies. This opens the nation up to crises of confidence and leadership

2/28/2020

DEATH

& TAXES

Jordan D. Weisinger, M.S., M.A., M.B.A

If the topic of this book is relevant, please respond with letterhead correspondence citing the title of the book in an interesting chapter. I have a growing collection of responses after the Sequestration Act of 2011 and near debt default of 2013.

CONTENTS

FOREWORD

The Red Queen is an evolutionary hypothesis where organisms must constantly adapt to circumstances that are also in a constant state to change, in order to gain reproductive advantages and survive. The more they evolve to meet the demands of their current environment, the faster their environment evolves to overcome them. The organism must constantly adapt in order to preserve their current position. Hence, it appears to be running in place. The Red Queen rules over the domains of biology and politics. States and nations are living organisms subject to the same competitive evolutionary environments other animals are. They must ceaselessly work at survival or they will be overcome by wealth inequality, corruption, or predictably brutalized by a neighbor. Just like in biology where successful organisms pass on their genetics, the more successful states and nations will pass on their public policy. This is more evident in democracies where their governance systems are more adaptive and responsive. A more dominant political party will win more elections and pass more laws. Really successful nations export their public policy and preferences through negotiated trade agreements, nation building and coalition formation.

Political ideologies also evolve as time passes and new environments emerge. Socialism is dying. Its centrally controlled industry might be acceptable for healthcare, policing, and other sensitive government-based services but it is the worst way to organize the overwhelming majority the economy. Communism was the most abhorrent political system to be tested to date, affecting the lives of hundreds of millions of persons. The fixed and despotic political outcomes ensured the centrally managed economies were not reformed or delivered equitably. The evidence is in and Communism is an abject failure. However, the rhetoric and idealization of socialism persists because Capitalism produces wealth inequality and poor justice system outcomes. Like a virus or some other adaptive system, democracy must incorporate the more successful elements of socialism to make it immune to movements seeking equality in outcomes rather than equality in opportunities. Econometric representation accomplishes this by adopting the   language and organizational aspects of socialism within the machinery of democracy. Instead of the proletariat monopolizing political power, they are permanently incorporated in the electorate and bicameral process.

By separating and isolating the below median class within its own legislative chamber, it empowers them with better role identity, stronger collective bargaining, and more agency from wage restricted political representatives. The proletariat is thus elevated by democracy, and set equal to the leisure class and investors class in the above median chamber. Democracy is by far the dominant process, but it learns from it experiences like other social or biological organisms. Democratic Socialism is the belief that socialism can be acquired through the Democratic process. Economic Representation builds this belief system into the machinery of the political process. The electorate can be split evenly into two equal parts, with one group comprised of those paying below median tax liabilities and another group comprised from those paying above median tax liabilities. This is the highest form of democratic entitlements as it perseveres majority rule and a bicameral process, while imbuing vectorized class identity within the legislature. The more specialized electorates will produce more honest representatives and more accurate and efficient public policy. This is how more specialized labor produces value for firms and it will be the same result for a more evolved political market.

Human biology is remarkable because a billion years ago our simplest cells merged with a virus called mitochondria, and it is only from this incorporation that we are able to survive. This is equivalent to the role specialization in a median partition based on class. Communism is a virulent and dangerous ideology but when it is stripped bare of its violent tendencies and collared within the democratic process, it will act as a source of motivation and power for the nation, much like mitochondria does for our most fundamental cells. Democracy will be forever changed by the median partition. It will be stronger, smarter, and more adaptable than its ancestors. It only needs outcomes to support these conclusions. The evidence needs to be derived from real world models, that swim, leap, fly, and run in the same economic and political environments more conventional democracies are found.

This is no easy ask, but if citizens of occupied nations are able to decide on the form of their own government during nation building exercises, many will choose a newer, more efficient, and more adaptable version of democracy. The other route is more tenuous, more tedious, and less certain. Contemporary democracies can reform their current institutions, or strike the older ones down to recreate a government closer to their own image, but this is more speculative and less certain. Both strategies require a leap of faith. Without prior examples, there will never be the pressing evidence needed to convince bureaucrats or activists that there exists a more perfect system.

Biology has performance measures for fitness such as reproduction rates, mortality rates, and longevity. Politics also has performance measures. They come in terms of GDP growth rates, satisfaction polls, electoral turnout. This is the science of politics. It can be captured in the discrete values that are recorded over time by individuals, firms, and governments. This does not capture all of the probabilities and possibilities inherent in a social organism like democracy. Some of it can be predicted from prior histories with known variables and unknown inputs, but a significant portion is never captured in the data. It is left to speculation and imagination.

The value of literature is in part evaluating and estimating outcomes that are possible but have not come to pass. There is value to predicting poor outcomes and then assessing the causes and presenting possible solutions. History tends to reoccur in predictable patterns. The same situation may arise with different outcomes possible. Literature is able to examine these alternate solutions to histories while they are still imaginary. The stated goal of this deliberation is to keep the worse outcomes imaginary by increasing the sanctions on behavior contributing to these poor outcomes. The intent is to develop a culture which recognizes or identifies these behaviors earlier and then commits to actions that avoid or change them. There will always be demonstrated value in assessing the inputs into an event, and then assessing the possible remedies to change output. This is why uncomfortable inquiries into the motives and consequences of events must continue to be scrutinized.

It is also the responsibility of government to investigate those outcomes which may not be preferable but where there is a statistically significant probability of occurring, despite any cultural or personal objections to the possibility. Government must assess the likelihood and then allocate resources to mitigate the threat. This includes low probability and high impact events. If a probability of just 2% was assigned to an event as catastrophic as a debt default or secession, the government should still investigate and prepare for the possibility, despite the lack of imminent danger. These calculations get more complicated when they depend on an electoral outcome that can vary wildly and oscillate from term to term. Although current conditions may not validate urgent concern, the loss of an election cycle may change the disposition of politicians and civil servants. Outside stimulus, like the business cycle, may also alter the trajectory of the nation, and this is hard to predict out from one term to the next.

This process becomes increasingly uncomfortable when it involves coworkers and neighbors, but when large numbers of voters support pubic policies like debt defaults and prolonged government shutdown, their preferences should not be discounted. These outcomes must not be underestimated because of the negative consequences but rather expected despite them. Populations usually pursue political outcomes which may contradict normative values or outcomes outside rational expectations, but this doesn't mean they are less likely, it only distributes incentives or outcomes less evenly. It is a lack of understanding or a deficit in perspective that contributes to the poor estimation of intent, when outcomes exceed the range of normal expectations.

Governments don't have the leisure to discount unproductive behaviors, they must immediately respond with public policy and preparation to mitigate the worst consequences of that behavior. This is easier to accommodate in federal systems, as states gain representational efficiencies with specific perspectives found within the electorate. Instead of relying on gross estimates of public perceptions or expectations on the federal level, states can specialize in a more precise interpretation of events or likelihoods. The states are more diverse and a larger number of possible outcomes or solutions can be considered. This will improve the quality of outcomes, especially if the consideration is priced into elections leading up to a possible event.

Predicting is often the easy part. Presenting solutions is the hard part. This book posits tax-based representation as the best means to protect against threats of debt default and government shutdowns. Tax-based systems of representation make democratic nations less susceptible to the threat of government shutdown and debt defaults by allocating more political representation to the states paying more federal taxes. This has two significant effects. The more populous and wealthier states generally prefer progressive taxes and this will result in lower deficits. Threats to shut down the government or default of its debt are less legitimate when the government takes on less accumulated debt and maintains smaller deficits. The states that generally pursue austerity measures and pursue government shutdowns most often will have significantly less representation in at least one of the legislature's chambers. This will reduce the number of attempts and seriously curtail the support for these dangerous policies. The combination of these two properties in tax-based representation will make nations more likely to survive into maturity, where higher per capita incomes and stronger labor rights, make the population far less susceptible to a culture of government shutdowns and debt default threats.

Despite the best laid out plans, it is impossible to predict the outcomes of elections held under a new system like income or tax-based representation. Not only are those electorates untested but each one will develop their own opposition party with different political preferences and voter turnout. Predicting Conventional elections are notoriously hard even with decades of histories to rely on. Econometric systems have no histories and predicting results is strictly speculative. However, certain themes are present in history and econometric system plays on those which tend to focus on those voters which are generally underrepresented in majoritarian democracies and conventional democracies. Form matters more than output, in respect to this book as it introduces a new paradigm derived from applying descriptive statistics and econometrics to institutions and electorates. It may change everything or nothing. Splitting the electorate into two adversarial parts may produce the same quality and frequency of laws in a majoritarian or conventional democracy.

However, the audacity of hope leads me to believe that improved role identity, a fiduciary duty, and the adversarial relationship between chambers will markedly improve the quality of labor laws for the poor and civil rights for minorities. This book Ileana expressly intended to improve the outcomes of demographic shifts and the plight of the poor and vulnerable citizens. Democracy is a living organism that must adapt new environments including demographic shifts, wealth inequality, and climate change. The old style of majoritarian politics will fail us in every respect. To have faith in the people is to understand they need support the support of institutions and rhetoric to explain the nuances of political power and economic advantage. Econometric systems of representation provide this extra benefit where conventional democracies languish.

Tax-based representation is intended to insulate the public from the most serious defects in due process by incentivizing a path towards progressive taxes and durable government. Debt default threats and government shutdowns are the most derisory risk to democracies and tax-based representation is the best protection against these insults. The more insults a government suffers, the more short-term thinking dominates public policy and electoral outcomes. This threatens the democratic nation and their neighbors. Tax-based representation allows the public the time they need to address wealth inequality, demographic shifts, and climate change without the persistent threat of default or shutdown.

Democracy is not yet done evolving, and econometric systems of representation will prove themselves to be an effective offshoot of demographic-based systems. These competing political are less adversarial and more complementary. Tax-based systems are compatible with other forms of democracy requiring no explicit choice to exclude one or favor another. Econometric systems come in enough variety to satisfies the organizational demands of most constituencies and sovereignties. At the very least, they will push contemporary democracies to their boundaries when trying to accommodate the anti-discrimination and anti-corruption properties of econometric systems. The goal is always towards a more perfect union, with high quality democratic entitlements distributed to the adult age population, without exclusion or disproportionate representation.

1 THE LANGUAGE OF REBELLION

The smell of rebellion is in the air. Not only does the United States suffer from rampant wealth inequality but it is in middle of historic demographic shift, where for the first time ever, a democracy will transfer majority political power from one demographic group to another. Most demographic shifts have resulted in pogroms or genocide, and the United States is presenting the telltale signs for the same outcomes. The nation is acquiring significant amounts of debt due to a relentless defunding of the federal government, and suffers almost yearly threats of government shutdowns or debt default threats. These two threats are the most effective way a political party can organize a revolt against a democratic government. As the number of insults increase, so does the likelihood of an event.

Debt defaults and government shutdowns pose a persistent threat in most presidential democracies because they require interventions to avoid. If any part of the process fails to pass a debt ceiling measure, the nation defaults. Most legislatures are bicameral and in competitive elections the control will be split between two or more parties. In other democracies, a president may have veto power over the bills. Too many things can go wrong. A debt default may be a reaction to a criminal investigation, a compromised election, or a simple miscounting of votes. It only takes one chamber or one principle for the unthinkable to occur. Defaults may also occur as a result or intent or negligence. The motivation for a debt default is far less important than the consequences.

The shutdown itself may incite a default without any actual vote held on a debt ceiling measure. A government shutdown is effectively a boycott on new legislation and that may include debt servicing and debt ceiling measures. If the legislature isn't meeting to pass a budget, and the shutdown persists for longer than the commitment to the last debt servicing measure, a lack of dedicated funds will provoke a default even if not overtly intended. If the government shutdown causes a debt default, the parties and pubic may not be able to assign blame. It will be a partisan conflict with people relying on tribalism for support. Worse, if a party was perceivable at fault, it will introduce a moral hazard. They won't want to reconstitute the government because they will almost certainly lose the next election. They will have every incentive to maintain the shutdown and move their leadership to the regional governments. This is an optimal environment for secessions or usurpations.

Once a default has occurred, it changes the political calculations made by all of the elected officers and voters. What was once a viable relationship between states and citizens, now becomes a burden. The debt serving costs could double, causing a huge increase in taxes. The securities markets and economy could crash, requiring even more government intervention or subsidy. Worse, voters will examine which states make the most contributions to the nation, and which receive the greatest subsidies. The political union will be viewed primarily in financial terms. The cost benefits analysis will exclude intangibles and those hard to measure aspects. One demographic group or political party will blame the other and conflict may ensue. What may have been negligence could result in civil war or dissolution.

A debt default followed by a government shutdown is the most effective way one party or demographic group can start a rebellion and win a civil war. Imagine a scenario where the government defaults on its debt and debt servicing costs double. Also imagine a massive correction in the economy that cuts tax revenues by 20% or increases spending by 20%. The government will already be struggling with a 40% change in revenues and expenses in an environment where borrowing is no longer an option. In the chaos, half of the states secede, cutting revenues by another 40-50%. Costs would effectively double while revenues shrink by half with no prospect of raising capital through the bond markets. Wars are incredibly expensive and could effective double the government's expenditures again.

A prolonged government shutdown could last as long as the full term of the representatives in the chamber that refused to pass a budget. In the United states, this is two years and more than enough time for the rebellious states to constitute a new interim government and raise an army from the national guard and local police forces. A federal government will be able to continue operating for a few weeks or months with emergency funds, but if the legislature refuses to pass a budget, the government will remain shut down. Eventually all borrowing authority will end and all funds exhausted. It is within these first two years, where the nation faces its most severe threat of secession or loss of democratic entitlements.

A few weeks into a prolonged government shutdown, the president will be reduced to a figurehead. They will have no means to enforce laws or fight wars. If the rebel legislators keep the government shutdown, the legislature cannot pass any new laws and pass any new budgets. The rebel legislators may remain in office and can obstruct any effort by the loyalists to reassert law and order over the Union. The legislature cannot act without them if no quorum can be met. The legislature cannot remove them. Nothing can compel a majority of legislators to pass any laws supporting the federal executive branch. This is true even if the rebel states are in open revolt against the government. The rebels can wait the full two years or until their interim government is established before declaring secession and retracting their representatives. If prosecuted in the correct order, there is virtually no recourse to a secession enforced by a government shutdown and debt default. Although, typically immoral and unpatriotic, this strategy is completely legal until the declaration of independence is made by the rebels.

Enlisted would start leaving the armed forces if the government could not pay their wages. It would also certainly be an incentive for less loyal soldiers to join the confederacy. The rebellious states will start diverting federal revenues back to their own balance sheets. Tax-holidays are more effective when state laws are passed, appropriating the payroll, sales, and income taxes collected by firms and large corporate businesses. This will allow them to staff up their local militias form from municipal police forces. Almost three quarters of an army may be support roles for front-line troops while police forces are almost entirely front-line operators. Often, the number of police officers employed by the local governments will be equal to the number of enlisted in a nation's standing army. They will be able to onboard the disaffected enlisted from the formerly federal government. In some nations, the state governments already manage veteran enlisted in National Guard units which can be up to 50% of the nation's front-line soldiers. These veteran troops will assume leadership over the veteran's police forces and effectively organize a formable force to defend territory or launch insurgency.

Whenever threats of debt default and government shutdowns are present, it requires a state-level response. In most simulations, the states will have priority to respond by resisting authoritarianism or by rebelling against the current administration. Federal systems of government include sovereignty for the state governments and they are granted full authority to act in all instances not covered by the constitution. A prolonged government shutdown is one of these circumstances. The federal government won't be able to marshal the financial resources, the labor resources, or good will it needs to put down a confederacy of states. If the government is shutdown, there is no appropriation authority to make purchases or meet payroll obligations. The federal government loses all borrowing authority and must rely on cash tax receipts. After the states start diverting revenues back to themselves, the federal government will be devastated financially and unable to enforce its laws.

The states will still have viable budgets and cash flows and the nation will depend on them to put down the rebellion or usurpation. Each state has its own borrowing authority and balance sheet, giving it access to the credit it needs to subsidize a war effort. The state government have significant veteran police forces and national guard armies to draw on, before they enact a draft or financial incentive to enlist. The states have to be aware of supply chains for military hardware, ensuring they have the arms and munitions to defend themselves. Supply chains will be disrupted, with many manufacturers using parts from other nations or states. Those states with ports have a huge advantage in that they can import new arms and munitions rather than build them. Every state should have an emergency plan in place should the federal government be shut down for an extended period. The states should have their own plans and not rely on plans determined by the defunct federal government. There is no downside to states maintaining these plans if the risk of default or shutdown is already present in the political environment.

Before any real violence started, the federal government would be crippled by a loss of revenues and debt servicing. The opposition force could sue for peaceful dissolution and it would be a more reasonable outcome than destroying the nation's GDP with bombing campaigns, urban assaults, and occupation. The former union is better off splitting into two new nations, discharging the debt acquired by the former government, and starting off in peace with a clean balance sheet and the benefit of a functioning economy. The two nations can then agree on immigration policies between them with trade resuming. It is not a best-case scenario but many nuclear armed nations will have no other recourse. They will have to accept a peaceful dissolution of face possible nuclear war with a nation sharing their border.

For non-nuclear armed nations, the combination of a debt default and economic ruin will greatly improve the effectiveness of local militia, veteran national guard armies, and defecting enlisted from the standing armies (air forces and navies included). The local sourcing of troops will allow the secessionists to deflect any attempt from the loyalist to forcibly preserve the territorial borders of the political union. Without nuclear annihilation to dissuade the two sides from violence, armed conflict is far more likely with a devastating effect on GDP and democratic institutions. Although the nation may have avoided secession or violence with more debate. Once the debt default and government shutdown occur, there will be fewer inhibitions to violence. Even if the right to secession is culturally accepted, the economy will already be in ruin and there will be less reason to avoid open warfare.

Government shutdowns pose the most significant risk to democratic governments for three reasons. First, they are the most effective method to divert funds away from the federal government back to the state governments. Most taxes are collected on the state and firm levels and can be easily redirected. Second, they prime the electorate to support the rebellion by coercing them into public commitments of support. Public declarations of support make the rebellion far more effective than any secretive coups or spur of the moment movement. Third, when rebellions are fomented on due process, it limits the options another party has to counteract it. On the surface, the rhetoric and policies are legitimate, serving the interests of their constituencies, which makes it more effective than outright declarations. Without historical references, this strategy for rebellion is less recognizable and nearly impossible to dispel or prevent. During this period neither the military nor the federal law enforcement can act while the government is shutdown, making it more dangerous than other crises.

Government shutdowns are one of the more serious insults a nation can suffer. Although most are short in duration, there is the possibility that it extends until new elections are held several years later. If the shutdown occurs immediately following an election, this could be a period of two-years or more. There is the expectation that the politicians will price the likelihood of winning subsequent elections into their determination to keep the government shutdown. The longer a government remains shut down by a party, the more likely they are to lose the next election. However, if the party has already determined to use this opportunity to organize a rebellion, they will care less about losing the next election cycle and the two-year delay between elections presents the best opportunity to mobilize the states in open revolt. State controlled national guard armies and local police forces may be enough to overwhelm a federal government is denied appropriations and borrowing authority. . War efforts costs substantial amounts of money and the states have an advantage if the government remains shutdown for one or two years before the next elections. After the states start diverting federal revenues collected by firms residing in their territories, the federal government will never fully recover, even after new elections.

No political party threatens debt defaults and government shutdowns unless they are comfortable with the worst-case outcomes resulting from those policies. The body politic should view these policies with suspicion every time they come up in discussion. They are telling of the incentives behind the threats: political parties worrying about demographic shifts will view debt defaults as a means to preserve sovereignty over themselves. This is especially true if they expect to have majority power in the states most likely to declare independence. If the party will predictably lose majority-demographic status in the larger nation, they will naturally emphasize state electoral outcomes and state rights over unity and voting rights

The secessionist party will want to maximize their probability of success. Not explaining their real intentions will help accomplish this goal. Older democratic systems are far more susceptible to crises of confidence or process, despite the public being completely unaware of the risks. It is the job of the majority party to explain the incentives and the consequences of a default prior to the crises so that the voter's price in these outcomes into elections prior to the event. It is not enough to attribute the threats of debt default or government shutdown to entropy or disorder. Political parties are made up of millions of persons and are fully capable of predicting or appreciating the consequences of their actions. Intent can't be obfuscated by mob rule and anarchy if preceded by very deliberate public policy preference. Otherwise, only history can distill the facts and circumstances leading to a default or dissolution. It is written by the political party and society that wins presenting the opportunity for a cover-up.

Most democracies dont have 100% of the public voting in 100% of the elections. Most democracies see only 70% voter participation, where a small minority of 35% can dictates public policy for the other 65%. In secession movements, a minority of voters could decide the future for a majority of persons during a single referendum or vote. This is also the strongest argument against secession movements. Even if a secession movement gains 51% majority, it would irreparably harm the other 49% who did not agree to the terms of separation. This makes most secession movement illegitimate from the very start. It is untenable that a small minority is able to force other residents to surrender their citizenship when citizenship is associated with economic benefits, civil rights, and voting rights. Not only will the minorities face almost certain incarceration risks and worse economic outcomes but there will be no expectations of improving conditions through due process. Without recourse, the minority populations are more likely to resist and protest.

The party seeking secession may be looking forward at a future where immigration and demographics will render them the minority party in national elections and subject to the executive and legislative authority of an emergent demographic group. A secession will allow the party to preserve their national identity and political hegemony. It is the best method an empowered minority has access to maintain power when they cut off support from the national parties preserving laws from passing to protecting their civil

8

rights, voting rights, and economic rights. The demographic majority can reduce the other political party to a permanent minority or worse, suppress their vote by incarceration and other anti-democratic policies. By separating themselves from a larger union, they can acquire more certain electoral outcomes and policy outcomes.

Debt default threats and government shutdown give the political caste and opportunity to dictate terms of secession during a crisis and create economic conditions that maximize chances of success. If the terms of the dissolution were spelled out in more certain outcomes, it would change the preference of both the voters and of the political caste. The economic consequences of a secession should be known before the public votes for that outcome in a referendum. Voters aren't likely to vote for dissolution, if their state budgets would take on a 20% deficit and where their economy loses an average of 3% in economic stimulus every year. An involuntary dissolution might result in trade barriers, tariffs, or economic sanctions that will certainly result in further disruptions to supply chains and new accounting and tax regimes.

An informed public would vote in their best interests and likely stand against a dissolution or secession. If they didn't, they will be less surprised when they lose their job, their home, or their voting rights after supporting the secessionist movement. At least they won't be able to blame the other states and other political parties for their own shortsightedness or terrible judgement. To make matters even worse, those residents forced into this precarious situation involuntarily will start protesting and maybe rioting. This invites the specter of demographic violence against minorities when the governments use institutional power to put down any dissent and restore order to a failing state. The state will be in economic free fall with dissenters everywhere looking to organize and protest the circumstances.

This is why it is incredibly important to identify these shifts in preferences or allegiances early. If this attitude can be diagnosed early, the threats and the consequences of debt defaults can be debated by voters, pundits, and elected officials. The people can price in the expectation of dissolution into electoral output. More importantly, if the public are more aware of the circumstances and consequences before an event, they will make better choices during the crisis. A larger portion of the population will continue to support the political union. The viability of the secessionist cause will decrease, as the number of states supporting the measures sinks. Information asymmetries benefit those seeking to forcibly secede while full disclosure benefits those states and citizens preferring to maintain the union.

One of the better indicators of the likelihood of an event are budget negotiations repeatedly timed to come immediately after elections. This is purposefully engineered to shut down the government for the maximum amount of time if the party does not like the outcome of the last election. This includes off year, mid-term, and presidential election years. In an environment where one party repeatedly threatens default or shutdown, the other party must reciprocate and time budget negotiations for elections where they stand to lose the most. Authoritarianism is often lurking in the looming shadow of reoccurring public finance crises, and minority parties must consider the threat of anti-democratic policies following an illegitimate election.

Parties must recognize the circumstances that make ordinary budget negotiations dangerous. Wealth inequality and demographic shifts can turn predictable arguments into constitutional crises and disasters. Silence is one of the best indicators of risk. When one party makes several obvious and aggressive moves during budget negotiations and the other party does not reciprocate, it is an indicator of weakness. The other party clearly recognizes the threat and are unable to predict or acquire adequate solutions. Their silence is a last-ditch effort to avoid a conflict they dont have a chance in winning.

Silence is the expression of dread. Dread causes hesitation and hesitation leads to poor outcomes. Only an informed electorate can pass the laws it needs to avoid a default or protect voting rights and civil rights. Only an informed electorate can price the risk into elections and avoid candidates who may harm them. Only an active electorate can discourage their political caste from participating in this dangerous behavior or supporting despots. The threat of election loss will make these representatives less likely to exploit budget processes or threaten default. An informed electorate will have the opportunity to look for any and all recourse to mitigate the risk. Democracies most important assets are due process and elections. These properties are the safest and most effective way to negotiate the circumstances contributing to a secession or war.

Outcomes can be improved by clearly describing the deleterious behavior as dangerous and malicious. The electorate will select better candidates in the primaries, vote for better candidates in the general elections, and rebuke politicians for pursuing threats and shutdowns. More importantly, the public will be more prepared for crises that require quick decisions. If silence is replaced with informed consent, the public would not be as susceptible to the public policies and posturing that make crises more likely. Silence only emboldens those who would take advantage of an uninformed public. Silence is an accomplice to those seeking to benefit themselves and preserve political power where they would ordinarily lose it.

An informed electorate provides one other significant benefit. The victors write history but it is far harder to cover up when the public and the media have formed strong opinions and gathered facts the corroborate alternative conclusions. The best defense against coercion, corruption, and complicity by a political caste is the development of relevant facts and strong histories that contradict any lies or mischaracterization of events after the crisis. Silence allows the party in power to dictate how perceptions leading up to the crisis are framed and how the media and academics describe the event afterward. Strong social and political pressures will force the voters to comport their expectations and memories to the new reality. Prosecution and economic ruin will scare away dissent as public opinion regresses to the new mean.

Where individuals do not have the authority or capacity to resist an illegitimate government, the political representatives in the legislature must commit to the use of institutional protests. A prolonged government shutdown may be the only recourse an opposition party has to prevent an authoritarian from consolidating power, ending civil liberties, and disrupting self-rule. Institutional protests are inherently lawful and the most effective strategy for coercing peaceful regime change. If a candidate refuses to vacate office after losing an election, the opposition party is expected to shut down the government until valid elections can be held. If the prior administration still refuses to leave office, the opposition party may consider a debt default and call up the state national guards to protect their protesting populations.

These may seem like drastic moves but if the opposition party does not act immediately by shutting down the government and calling up the national guard, they risk legitimizing the authoritarian regime. If the opposition party hesitates, they may see other anti-democratic policies enacted and the less likely future elections will cure the rot of despotism. Court rulings may be disregarded, laws may remain unenforced, and election winners may not be seated. The longer the opposition party waits to respond, the worse their chances of overcoming authoritarianism and preserving democracy. The more patient they are, the fewer allies they will have in the military and civil service, to rely on when the people rise up against the authoritarian regime. The states that do protest at a later date, risk being occupied and losing their voting rights entirely. If they don't all act as one in the first moments of the crisis, they can expect to be inevitably converted to despotism one by one.

Any effort on part of the executive to circumvent the authority of the legislature must be viewed as authoritarian and anti-democratic. It must be resisted by the entire legislature and all of the regional executives. Most legislatures have the unchallenged right to shut down the government with no recourse through the courts or executive branch. This is the power of an institutional protest. This is the ultimate check on an executive who doesn't respect the law or election cycle. It is a peaceful way to prematurely end the regime of an authoritarians or illegitimate president. It is also easily resolved. If the next election is determined to be valid, or all parties vacate the office if expected, budget negotiations may resume and the regular course of business can be pursued.

2 INPUT EQUALS OUTPUT

Politics is tribal. During crises we rely on family histories, networks or friends and coworkers, and we fear reprisals from employers or local politicians. In this environment it rarely matters who causes a shutdown or is in control when emergency powers are evoked, the nation will break down into sectarian motivations and allegiances. The risk of loss is so great that prior relationships are less valuable than a guarantee of safety in an unsafe environment. Most times, blame is for the historians to record and history is written from the perspective of the winning tribe or party. This usually benefits the majority demographic group, which are also more likely to favor government shutdowns and threats of default. They are typically the land owners, the firm owners, and are more likely to occupy the executive branch with a majority of the electorate. This is one reason why demographic violence is so frequent. It is incredibly effective, with most of the arithmetic favoring them. A superiority in numbers is a useful tool when attrition rates can change the electorate in their favor.

One of the leading indicators of demographic instability is wealth inequality. Wealth smooths over many of the obstacles to political power a waning demographic group fear. It allows them to retain power for much longer if they relied exclusively on fair and open elections. Corruption quickly follows wealth inequality and this will result in weakened law enforcement and oversight. When corruption through deregulated campaign finance and partisan redistricting fails, the outgoing demographic majority will pursue voter suppression, mass incarceration, and other anti-democratic policies to preserve power. The use of institutional abuses predisposes the majority-demographic group to the use of more extreme violence like pogroms and war.

Austerity measures will exacerbate wealth inequality by eroding the culture supporting progressive estates taxes and income taxes. Without progressive estates taxes, wealth accumulates in a small number of well capitalized corporations. These firms monopolize the securities markets and dominate commerce. These owners can entrench themselves in the political process through campaign finance and the promise of future employment and wealth. The concentration of political power makes it harder to pass more egalitarian and sounder tax policies with economic reforms. This is when authoritarians will seek to exploit the weakened political system and pass anti-democratic policies to consolidate and preserve political power.

The majority-demographic group will often horde the wealth of a nation through exploitative economic policies. They maintain a near complete control over the largest companies in the country, preserving a monopoly on the labor and capital. For this reason, the demographic majority will advocate for policies like weak labor laws, low taxes, and poorly regulatory environments. They will relentlessly pursue austerity measures that keep the government under-capitalized and under-utilized. They will refuse to raise taxes to correct the wealth inequality and keep the government buried under deficits and debt. The margin for error increases as the number of options available to the government diminish during a crisis. When conditions deteriorate, the threat of aristocracy or despotism looms over the formerly democratic nation.

No party makes threats of default lightly. They are aware of the consequences. The very presence of this rhetoric is a threat of civil society and democracy. A debt default is part of a long-term strategy of a demographic-majority to keep and preserve power despite their status being challenged by the high birth rate or immigration rate of a minority population. It is the best indicator that the demographic-majority will try to secede or usurp power while they still have dominant demographic, economic, and political positions. Once the rhetoric of debt defaults and shutdowns are accepted by the public it is near impossible to root it out without reforms that require the demographic majority to agree to them.

No short-term outcomes will satisfy the waning majority-demographic group in the long term while their political power diminishes and the options, they have to retain power dwindle. Although the minority demographic groups can accept austerity and budget cuts in the near term, there will be other periods in which the deficit grows and debt accumulates. Unless the rhetoric is soundly defeated and put permanently to rest, the majority-demographic group will have other opportunities to organize a rebellion around a debt default or government shutdown. Most demographic shifts last several decades, eroding the ability to predict or prevent them. The minority party politicians will forget the past and unlearn everything taught to previous generations. This will cause them to hesitate or retreat when discipline and courage are needed the most. This is one more reason why history has the tendency to repeat itself so often.

It is possible a political party develops blindness in regards to possible outcomes. Political parties may not consider the consequences of an event or probability of it occurring if they don't have a recent experience to reference. The public is notorious for under-estimating the likelihood of something happening if it hasn't happened yet during their lifetimes. Generations that may have faced similar circumstances start to die off and the nation loses its community resistance. More likely, the terrible consequences produce stress that disincentivize individuals to discuss it with immediately family, relatives, friends, and coworkers. If poor outcomes are predictable and unavoidable, the opposition party will likely resort to denying the likelihood of an event in a last-ditch effort to reduce the risk of the other political party acting on the opportunity.

If a culture of debt defaults threats and government shutdowns persists for more than just a few years, the odds of an event increase as parties become less tolerant and more brazen in their negotiations. Political parties are people and when outcomes don't match their expectations they will get upset and react rashly. When the parties are fixated on debt default threats and government shutdowns, it creates an incredibly dangerous environment where conflict is only one vote or election away. The parties may become more homogenous making the likelihood of a mistake more likely. If they all come to the wrong conclusion, there is no one to contradict or challenge them. More importantly, the economic or demographic circumstances may change resulting in more incentives or opportunities to launch a successful secession or usurpation. Each year is a new opportunity for disaster, with the number and dispositions of representatives changing.

There will be little recourse for an opposition party that does not defend the nation against threats of default or budget shutdowns. They can't price the consequences of an event into prior elections, and are not likely to successfully defend the nation during an event. The opposition party will be forced to accept the outcomes of an event they barely participated in. Worse, they will only have themselves to blame for not adequately characterizing the consequences and giving themselves an opportunity to pass the laws needed to avoid a catastrophe.

After a default, unemployment will skyrocket, and the labor force participation rate plummet. A large portion of disaffected persons will have too much free time to dwell on the causes of the debt default. They will swell with anger and blame immigrants, minorities, and women. They will be corralled by propaganda and demagogues into protecting and preserving the party that caused the default and economic recession. The demographic-majority will accept a leader that resembles them in religion, skin color, and persuasion. They will permit more unscrupulous behaviors if they believe it will help them preserve their political power and position as the owners class.

If the party causing the default has control over the presidency, they will put down the protests and riots that result from the damaged economy. Demographic majorities may also resort to violence to protect their monopoly on wealth and political power. Pogroms are common and they can devastate communities through death or loss of property. A pervasive environment of violence and disdain will permeate all aspects of society. The more the military and police are used to put down social movements, the more the people will grow to resist. Wide scale conflict is also a risk. Eventually, the president will seek permanent interventions and war power. This opens the door to despotism.

If 70% of the nation is one demographic group and 30% represents minorities, and if they inflict an equal number of casualties during war, the magnitude of loss is nearly twice as severe for the minority groups. This makes demographic violence a highly effective means of controlling the electorate for the majority demographic group. There is even more risk in civilian deaths, where indiscriminate bombing or extrajudicial killings exacerbate the losses to minority groups in territories controlled by the offending party. Democracies will predictably form political parties that separate into more homogenous and heterogenous groups, and this could disguise the demographic-based motivations in partisan conflict over deficits and electoral outcomes.

Demographic groups losing majority status will prefer policies that increase the level of entropy and disorder in the system. If there is a failure, they are far more likely to end up in a superior position. The majority demographic group is able to absorb more losses with little to no electoral impact. Minority groups often suffer twice the electoral impact of a majority demographic group making it far more profitable for a demographic group to rely on violence. Majority demographic groups also monopolize the wealth and resources of a nation making them far more likely to prosecute a successful war for usurpation or secession.

The majority-demographic party need not actually default to win. The party can use a filibuster or strategies to obstruct the legislature while repeatedly underfunding the federal government to preserve the wealth inequality and susceptibility to default threats. By preserving these conditions, they can ensure poor people have no recourse to challenge firms that exploit them or states that oppress them. By preserving these conditions, the majority demographic continues to divert incomes and wealth to their families rather than minority households. The federal government is perpetually at risk for a shutdown or default, allowing the majority-demographic group to prevent a peaceful transfer of political power. If a democratic nation can't effectively regulate itself or tax itself, it is equivalent to despotism. Instead of political despotism, the nation succumbs to industrial despotism. Large firms and the wealth. The threat of political despotism is merely delayed, until it is challenged giving the majority-demographic group an opportunity to install an authoritarian. thy fill the void left empty by the filibuster and legislative obstruction.

Opposition parties can identify these intentions years in advance. Arguments for default and threats of government shutdown are vocal and must be repeated yearly. The opposition party can easily protect itself with public policy and debate. They must examine the prospect of default and secession and explain the consequences to the public. If they respond quickly enough, debate is their most effective tool. If the consequences are deleterious, the public will reject the prospect and support the opposition party. Nothing is guaranteed but it does improve the likelihood of preserving the union and discouraging support for default. This strategy increases support for raising taxes to reduce the deficit. The levers of control that make a default plausible must be eliminated.

Don't underestimate the power of majority demographic party to preserve support by constituents in the period leading up to an event and just after it. There are many examples of majority demographic groups supporting candidates despite their pursuit of anti-democratic polices and aggregated economic exploitation. They continue to support partisan redistricting polices, voter suppression policies, and campaign finance laws that maximize the likelihood of their remaining in power after declining into minority party status. This primes the majority- demographic group for authoritarianism by coercing them into public commitments of polices that oppress and exploit minorities. It sets expectations that if the minority groups will resist, they will be met with violence as their protests are forcibly put down. Their support of these policies before conflict will balance with their continued support after conflict.

If the minority party starts to win majorities, or pass progressive taxes and anti-corruption policies, the majority-demographic group may act on their threats. If the event includes a debt default or prolonged government shutdown, the ensuing crisis afterward will convince them to stay the course and remain in support. They will start making all of the decisions in the basis of religion, race, and money. One of the more terrifying realities of a demographic shift, is that almost all of the electoral outcomes support the majority demographic group. On face value, they will win most elections: gubernatorial, senatorial, and presidential elections all use state-wide elections to determine the winners and in majoritarian elections. A demographic majority with a 51% margin will still win 100% of the elections in hyper partisan electoral environments.

The potential for a debt default and secession is found within the error term and the majority demographic group can excuse it by negligence or ignorance. If they are unaware of the consequences of their actions, they can't be held accountable by voters beforehand. If the attitude and agenda can't be cured through debate and due process, there may be too-few minorities remaining after a conflict to influence elections afterward or hold the majority demographic group accountable for their deleterious actions. With no accountability before an event, and likely no accountability after an event, there are very few disincentives to discourage the majority demographic group from pursuing dangerous and destructive path.

A premediated debt default would cause a terrible economic crisis shortly after it is announced. The insult could destroy stock market, bond markets, and credit markets. It even may cause hyperinflation. In addition to expenditures being twice that of revenues after a debt default and secession, money would devalue when borrowing is impossible and the government would have to rely on printing money. The government, will be forced into more budget austerity with huge cuts to welfare and other forms of economic stimulus. These conditions will paralyze corporate firms hiring and buying decisions.

The insult to the economy will cause profit margins to fall and joblessness to rise precipitously. If the public was not already susceptible to white supremacy, fascism, or aristocracy in its prior environment, they will soon be openly debating the topics. Violence offline follows long periods of economic strife and it is always accompanied by a rise in extremism and other dangerous ideologies. People look for certainty during crises and authoritarianism provides those outcomes. If the majority demographic can control more of the variables into economy and politics, they will make more concessions on civil liberties and economic output.

Debt defaults and government shutdowns are only risks to democracies. Despotic nations aren't threatened by discontented minority parties. Elected officials don't negotiate budgets or raise taxes. There is no chance of user error or opportunity for rebellion. The authoritarian controls all aspects of government, thus their biggest risk is in economic collapse and civil unrest. Democracies introduce user error into the budgetary process and rely on tradition rather than rules to protect themselves. Despots don't respect rules or tradition and can easily circumvent internal budgetary processes. This makes democracies more susceptible to regime change and internal conflict. Nearly 45% of the world qualifies as democracy but only 12% are considered high-quality democracies[1]. Almost 38% are despotic or authoritarian and immune to debt defaults. This leaves nearly half of the world's nations exposed to the risk. Low-quality democracies suffer from weak institutions and corruption. They may experience unchecked wealth inequality and suffer violence when demographic shifts occur.

Rebellion is a dangerous prospect for democracies. They carry far more risk than most suspect. They are rarely

---

[1] Democracy Index 2018: Me too?, page 2, The Economist Intelligence Unit, retrieved from www.eiu.com

successful and the consequences are almost always ruinous economy. Any attempt at rebellion is more likely to result in another authoritarian assuming control or the nation rather than a minority party successfully challenging a majority party pursuing ant-democratic policies. Democracies defending themselves against the creep of authoritarianism and corruption are much better off patiently seeking reform rather than launching into default and regime change. However, institutional protests may be the only way to dislodge an authoritarian from office. Coercing regime change peaceably through government shutdowns is a lawful and effective way to protect voting rights and civil rights.

Most rebellions will occur when a party or region seeks recourse through a secession. If they purse a policy of debt defaults and government shutdowns, they will have to broadcast their intent years in advance as they communicate their intent to colleagues and voters. It will remain innuendo until after the event occurs. The silence and secrecy maximize support for the debt default and shutdown policies. A much smaller portion of the population would support a debt default or shutdown if they thought it would result in a secession. A far larger portion of the population will support a secession after the default has occurred. The parties and the citizens will be blaming each other and looking for scapegoats. Tempers will flare and the viability of the nation will wane. A government is essentially a financial organization and when it ceases to be able to pay it obligations, it will cease to have the support of the people. When the people expect the nation to fail, they will look for leadership on the state or local levels.

A debt default is the most devastating way to announce independence but it may not be the most likely. Government shutdowns over budgets are far more likely to result in conditions that result in conflict. Budgets generally have to be passed every year giving ample opportunity to opposition parties and majority parties to use them as leverage in an event. Most governments can't function without a passed budget. Tax revenues continue to be collected, but the government has no authority to issue payments. A prolonged government shutdown effectively ends the tenure of the body. Most shutdowns are only a few days in length but they can last several months or years. If a party was committed to prematurely ending a federal government, they could shut it down until new elections are held several years later.

If a government continues to draw money from the treasury and pay its employees, it is an act of rebellion. It can be criticized as authoritarian and may be viewed as the first step towards despotism. In most democracies, the power over the purse is found in the legislature and any act circumventing the institutional protest is inherently undemocratic. Without a budget, a majority of the decisions will be made on the state or regional level. This is extremely dangerous as there is no guarantee of consensus or cooperation. The lack of national leadership imparts the marginal positions held by governors more authority and legitimacy, regardless of the consequences. Outcomes matter and a prolonged budget shutdown can shift the power downward to regional governments in the vacuum of a shuttered national government. This will destabilize even those nations with long histories of solidarity and unity.

Shutting down the government is the best strategy to sow dissent and create the dangerous conditions where a majority of citizens support emergency measures to suppress minorities actively resisting the regime. A shutdown may also be the pretense for a power grab. The executive may invoke emergency powers during a shutdown despite being the cause of the shutdown. It is a high probability play for an executive to grab power and avoid an election loss or arrest. This is similar to how the Reichstag fire was used to demand emergency powers to prevent other democratic institutions from failing.

Emergency powers represents one of the biggest risks to the democratic process because a large portion of the population will consent without any significant thought to the consequences. They may be described as necessary and temporary, but when they are combined with government shutdowns to the discretionary sectors of the government, they will likely result in permanent and substantial reductions in government services or protections. The suspension of government services will likely provoke protests and riots, resulting in the delay or end to democratic elections. All citizens must be wary of emergency powers following unresolved budget disagreements where large portions of the government are considered wasteful, unnecessary, and are ultimately shutdown.

The very presence of government shutdowns and threats of default are enough to verify suspicions that a party is considering secession or usurpation. Rational actors won't threaten a democratic government with harm, unless they benefit from disrupting elections and due process. The risks and consequences of a default or prolonged shutdown are simply too great. Any party repeatedly making threats has already considered the consequences, making the acts premeditated. The possibility of violence against the electorate should not be viewed as a byproduct of their negligence, but more of an ambition.

3 RECIPROCITY AND RETRIBUTION

Game theory is the complex mathematics behind relationships and decisions. Strategies are tested against each other through simulations or experiments with different strategies employed to maximize point gains. One variation in experimental game theory assigns different point values to the players depending on their use of an aggressive strategy or a cooperative strategy. If one player uses an aggressive strategy when the other player uses a cooperative strategy, the aggressive player wins the most points possible for a given game while the cooperative player wins zero. If both players pursue a cooperative strategy that each win a moderate number of points. If both players pursue an aggressive strategy neither wins any points. Each player participates in a number of separate games and tallies their points at the end. The results often depend on which are the dominant strategies used during the competition.

If there are a large number of aggressive players, the total number of points scored by all players is higher but there are significantly fewer winners. Most points are concentrated in a few players and the cooperative players have much smaller totals. If the majority of players employ cooperative strategies, then the total number of points won is lower but there are a larger number of winners. The aggressive players will have the least points. When scientists studied optimal strategies pursued by A.I., it demonstrated that the most successful strategy was reciprocity. The A.I. will always start off as cooperative but whenever there is aggression it will reciprocate. This strategy is called Tit for Tat and it maximized the points earned when interacting with both the cooperative and aggressive strategies.

Political markets are similar to game theory experiments. When political parties are more cooperative, they pass more economic reforms, more financial revaluations, and there are less threats of catastrophic interventions. More of the players in the economy and society have higher standards of living and society as a whole benefit. When one party pursues more aggressive, they can maximize returns for a smaller group in the economy, usually a racial group or the owners' class, and there are a smaller number of winners. The more competitive economic environment changes the individual strategies for voters, and they may use more aggressive strategies in the aggregate. This will make create wealth inequality and may result in less accurate electoral systems. The environment will be less equitable systems, reinforcing winner take all attitudes where the more aggressive parties win more often.

Results from game theory experiments will help political parties assess their current actions in regards to the average output across a number of different solutions. They can predict how effective their current strategy is compared to alternative strategies. Often, one strategy produces great results under optimal conditions but produces terrible results under worst-case or ordinary conditions. An average is taken, to accommodate for all of the known unknowns, unknown unknowns, and known knowns. The variables include economic conditions, electoral output, probability of anti-democratic polices being enforced, and then of course the likelihood of events like compromised elections, debt defaults, and permanent government shutdowns. Democracy with competitive elections make electoral output less predictable which in turn impacts which interventions are available for the parties to force a regime change, rebel, or resist an authoritarian. A strong position in one election cycle does not guarantee a strong position after the next election cycle. This is the wager majority and minority parties make. It is a riskier during periods of wealth inequality and demographic shifts.

Political parties must assess these situations with Nash equilibrium. They must look at the average outcomes and outlier outcomes, with worst case scenarios weighted appropriately. Often, a worst-case scenario will force a reaction by the opposition party, despite the low likelihood of permanent damage done to the democratic institutions. The risk of inaction far exceeds the risk of over-stepping in a protest. If the protest is lawful but unnecessary, there will be no other complications than a loss of elections or prestige. if the opposition party fails to act when an authoritarian first consolidates power, they may never get another chance as governors are replaced, legislators are arrested, and due process ceases to function.

Politics is not always a winner takes all game. One party may not be able to win but they could still lose in different degrees. They could lose their civil rights, economic rights, and voting rights. A union of 50 states could lose 20 or 30. There are a number of low quality but much more likely outcomes when evaluated in terms of more competitive political markets. Often a loss for one party is a gain for another and the worst outcome for one is usually the best outcome for the other. The greater the point differential the less likely that result will be acquired in an informed environment. These simulations are just estimations. An incredible amount of effort and courage are needed to acquire even average outcomes. If one party is more aggressive when the other party hesitates, it changes the weighted average in favor of the party demonstrating more capacity or interest in winning.

A single game takes all outcomes into consideration and assigns a value to each permutation. The strategy that acquires the highest average outcome over a series of games is the most appropriate strategy to pursue, even if the most likely outcome is loss. For national parties, losses may include the secession of states or the genocide of residents. The two outcomes are not exclusive. If some states secede, there will no opportunity for the other states to intervene and prevent losses of political rights or murders occurring in those break-away regions. It's even more complicated than it appears. The act of forcibly preventing states from seceding, to avoid possible future genocide, actually creates the opportunity for those states to make the demographic changes necessary to preserve majority power in a democracy. Wars can cause population collapse through causalities to enlisted and civilian deaths. A 10% reduction in population could preserve the majority-demographics political power for decades. These scenarios are often no-win situations, where leaders have to weigh two unacceptable outcomes against each other and select the one that benefits more over citizens, looking at both short term and long-term goals.

Don't underestimate the fact, that population is an interval level variable that can be altered with incarceration and murder. Interventions can change the democratic equation for entire nations or just a handful of its states. This is another no-win situation, where the only acceptable product is a non-event. The problem with this outcome is war is often not reciprocal. If one side is nearly certain to lose, the other side is guaranteed to win. Clearly, they side expected to win is more likely to force an event even when the other party does not consent. The minority party should not exclusively pursue optimized outcomes, or they risk putting themselves in an inferior position for most of the possible outcomes. If conflict is still the most likely outcome, a strategy that seeks only the optimized outcome will earn the worst returns.

The preferred strategies of A.I. in these experiments justify reciprocal debt default and shutdown threats, timed around elections as means to develop culture of support. If only one party makes the threats and the other party only uses it in emergencies, the more patient party runs the risk of not being supported. The more aggressive party, using the threats will win more elections, more public policy arguments, and more judicial appointments. They will also have the support of a larger portion of the public if they actually act on that threat. If the opposition party rarely reciprocates, and the language and arguments are not explicitly spelled out, the run the very real risk of being criminalized or losing the subsequent election. The party that works on the language of rebellion, develops a culture where it is expected and supported, will have advantages in war and suffer no consequences in short term electoral outcomes.

The preferred strategies of A.I. also take into account the propensity for retribution. Strategies that learn to retaliate against aggression must also be quick to forgive and forget those transgressions. The best strategies will reciprocate aggression only when aggression is present and then retreat back to cooperation as quickly as possible. This minimize the losses when facing more aggressive rivals while maximizing the points gains in more cooperative environments. Don't forget, rivals are learning and adapting. If they are taught, they can't win with aggression, they will accept cooperative environments. Political parties must retaliate when faced with aggression but cooperate when the opportunity arises. Cooperation is easier after a few election cycles, where incumbents lose and new politicians are elected.

This flexibility in the electoral process is also a source of extreme risk. In an environment where one party repeatedly threatens debt defaults or shutdowns, the rapid change in newly elected politicians also signals risk. The party making the threats may have less intent to act on them in the short term, the economic conditions and political conditions could significantly change resulting in a much greater future risk. The future is discounted by uncertainty that can't be predicted. The same attribute that makes political parties more likely to forgive and forget, also maximized the risk of catastrophe as politicians inculcate to the same risky behavior in dramatically different environments. Periods of demographic shift and wealth inequality qualify as conditions which could provoke debt defaults and government shutdowns even when the threat was previously present but not acted on.

Not all political parties optimize their strategies like Artificial Intelligence in Machiavelli styled experiments. Political parties may try to optimize results by suppressing information and moderating their rhetoric despite an escalation by the other party. This is a terrible strategy and will likely result in the worst outcomes. When the voters can't price in the information, elections are less competitive and the more moderate party can find themselves out of office and in the minority. Now, a more extreme and fundamentalist party occupies the presidency, with majorities in the legislature, and the opposition party in the minority and unable to defend itself. Suppressing information and moderating the rhetoric optimizes the outcomes for the other party. Game theory suggest that optimal results are acquired by reciprocating attitude and actions when developing strategies to maximize points, and this includes timing government shutdowns after elections in anticipation of preventing authoritarianism.

A party that is too conciliatory and cooperative, loses the majority at times when faced with more aggressive opponents, unless they have a clear structural majority. If they are in the minority, typical of most demographic shifts, they won't be able to depend on the numerical superiority of a more cooperative environment. The current majority-demographic group will win more elections and have more opportunities to achieve outcomes in their benefit. Even if elections are split between the two parties, this means the more aggressive party will win half posing an imminent risk. During the cycles where they win the Presidency, there will be an increased risk of authoritarianism, and during the cycles they win a simple majority in one of the legislatures, there is an increased risk of default, shut down, and secession. The minority-demographic groups suffer these risks in most electoral outcomes. Overly-cooperative parties reduce the odds they are able to defend themselves while in an inferior executive position, while not improving their ability to defend against a threat while they are in a superior position. Retaliation increases the odds of conflict but reduces the odds of a complete loss. Leaving it up chance is a terrible strategy to prevent authoritarianism and protect minority populations from murder and incarceration.

Game theory demonstrates that more aggressive individuals and parties do better in more aggressive environments. These environments can be predicted by the popularity of austerity measures, rapid debt accumulation, mass incarceration, voter suppression, deregulated campaign finance, and the lack of effective labor laws and progressive taxes. These economies and justice systems are harsher and suggest the cooperative parties will lose more often. Parties that favor despots and authoritarians thrive in more competitive environments. There is less trust in the media, elections, and democratic institutions. There is more reliance on family and closed social networks with voters aligning on racial terms even when not expressly stated. It is in this context, where threats of debt default and government shutdowns can cause a premature end to the game, with all of the points already allocated to the more aggressive players. The parties can easily predict a redistribution of the points if more cooperative parties are given an opportunity to pass progressive taxes and raise wages. An end to the game will prevent this possibility and this may be incentive enough for political parties in decline.

Political parties must be willing to accept suboptimal outcomes to avoid the worst-case outcomes. This takes courage. Political parties won't want to acknowledge the real risks out of fear it will contribute to the possibility of an event. When these likelihoods remain undisclosed, it increases the risk of over-committing to strategies that result in poor outcomes. This includes the worst-case scenarios from surrender to collaboration. However, suboptimal outcomes are much more likely once the parties become active in their own defense. Parties may position themselves for the irrational expectation of optimal outcomes prior to an event and change preferences after the event. Passing priority to the more aggressive party does increase the risk of having an event and decrease the quality of outcomes associated with that event, but it also it maximizes the opportunity for peaceful dissolutions or other nonviolent remedies outside of surrender or collaboration.

Seeking the optimal outcome rather than the most likely outcome increases the risk of despotism in another way. Optimized strategies will be conflict adverse, overly patient, and too complacent when faced with legislative obstruction. The lack of high-quality laws is equivalent to political despotism where the public may continue to elect representatives but they are unable to regulate or tax themselves. The optimized strategy will discount most behaviors or tactics that cause conflict. Any conflict could result in scenarios with unacceptable outcomes. Obviously, the issue is that most other outcomes are excluded as possibilities and the party finds itself pursuing the least likely set of outcomes.

The more complacent political party will moderate their own behavior, trying to earn these unlikely outcomes, and lose support from the moderates, putting the party in an inferior position when the environment becomes harsher and more competitive. They will be viewed as the weaker party and a larger number of residents will support the other more aggressive party because it makes it far more likely they survive a conflict or earn economic benefits associated with affiliation. In an environment of wealth inequality and political corruption, the waning demographic-majority could continue to win enough elections to continue obstructing legislation and threating default or secession to preserve a superior position.

Often parties will pursue the optimized strategy out of desperation, when all of the other strategy result in unacceptable outcomes. If conflict results in genocide or ethnic cleansing, a significant portion of the minority party will accept any terms offered by the majority-demographic group. The owners class is the primary beneficiary during this period. In a poor regulatory and low tax environment, they can continue to abuse labor and resources maximizing profits and personal wealth. When the minority party seeks optimized outcomes by avoiding conflict, it is rewarded and reinforced by campaign contributions and support in the business community. This contributes to the miasma of corruption by making future regulation or taxes less likely. Not only will they lose a majority of the elections but more of their members will be resistant to change. The owners class acquires a low-quality democracy, with virtually no regulation or taxation, without actually declaring support for despotism, or imposing it through debt defaults and government shutdowns.

There are good reasons for a political party to reciprocate the threat of default and government shutdowns. Their presence is an indicator that the same party will pursue anti-democratic polices while in office to remain in office. If the opposition party is unwilling to stand up for themselves against the threats of shutdown, they will hesitate when elections are interfered with, patiently wait out periods of voter suppression, and accept environments of abject corruption. The biggest risk is that they will join the establishment and put down public dissent as the nation slides into authoritarianism. Within just a few years, an authoritarian can assume power and consolidate power. Unless the opposition party is willing to reciprocate when the threat first becomes apparent, there may very little they can do after the fact when civil liberties are weaker and voting rights already compromised.

If the opposition party runs away from their obligations to their constituents, they will lose elections and they will be in a far weaker position. They may never recover enough and gain a majority in the legislature, making it impossible to threaten institutional protests in the future. This is why reciprocity is so critical. It primes the electorate for conflict by providing them context. It gives them the language and the legal arguments to defend themselves. More importantly it keeps them engaged. A better educated electorate is a more responsible electorate and they will feel empowered to intervene through elections and public policy. If the defects in the economy and political process can be cured, conflict and authoritarianism can be avoided. If the opposition party does not explicitly stand up against the slow decline of the democratic process with debate and policy, they will be observers to history, rather than the principals.

It is all about tolerance for risk, and if the leadership of the opposition party does not recognize the risk of an authoritarian regime, they will not resist it. It is a complicated decision, they may overemphasize the risk of property loss, incarceration, or death. Threats of violence are very persuasive strategies to get an opposition party to comply to the new regime. The politicians may under-emphasize the risk after pricing in expectations of collusion or cooperation. There are fewer personal consequences if they don't resist the new authoritarian regime. These are inputs into the decisions each individual politician makes alone in the absence of oversight and accountability. The disposition of the party will reinforce those conclusions: if nobody says anything or does anything, others will look around and model their behavior off of this outcome. The fear is contagious.

Silence and inaction are easier to reconcile with negligence and doubt. It is more excusable, especially there is no accountability after the loss of civil liberties and media eliminates possibility of criticism. And dissent When the opposition party fails to reciprocate threats of default, it is vectorized information demonstrating the tendency for the party to cooperate with the new authoritarian regime. The direction and speed of the nation's decline will be directly proportional to the ability and interest of the opposition party to protect civil liberties and voting rights. If the opposition party chooses to protect their own profits and preserve their own lives over the safety of their constituents, the rate of decline will accelerate. The opposition party will be under incredible stress to intervene but it is easier to hesitate and patient wait for the situation to resolve itself. Their inaction has consequences.

History does not reflect kindly on those parties and officials that cooperate with authoritarians, but these alternative histories are only found in democratic societies that don't censure dissent or history. These facts will only live outside of the nation with little impact on the new regime and the culture that revolves around it. Those politicians that barter away the civil liberties and voting rights of their constituents will otherwise live long and prosperous lives, filled with abundance and mirth, as long as they keep quiet and support the establishment. Outcomes are often obfuscated by the lack of conflict and the deteriorating conditions in a democracy and may not be expressed for decades. The quality of democratic entitlements may erode in one generation and then be implicitly accepted by the next generation. If they don't protest loudly at the start of decline, it is unlikely they protest later when the odds of successfully defending themselves are lower.

A lack of legislative production should be associated with political despotism when both result in the same product. There is a reason why the two are nearly equivalent. Most low-quality democracies often fall into despotism when challenged and this is an acceptable outcome for a waning demographic group seeking to maintain majority political power despite the change in demographics. All democratic nations suffer the risk of a slow decline into corruption and despotism if the majority demographic group is unchecked by the emergent demographic group. This is especially true for older presidential democracies.

Non-democratic nations aren't susceptible to opposition parties gaining majorities in the legislature and forcing a default or government shutdown. Autocratic counties are susceptible to popular revolts or elite regime change, but they always operate in secrecy with few resources and scant chances to succeed. Opposition parties can't act overtly and petition the business community and public for support. There is also no due process to protect citizens from abuse during investigations. With no legal protections, they will have to cooperate more often to avoid the worse sanctions. With no rights, their personal property and data is more accessible for investigations. This makes non democratic nations more durable than democratic nations.

This is an attractive outcome for businesses that like to control labor inputs and limit compensation to non-management employees. Non democratic nations are less likely to pass intrusive regulations which would otherwise lower profits and disrupt production efficiencies. Corporations often have revenues larger than small companies and highly expert labor forces. Most corporations are not democratic. They are more like little feudal fiefdoms, where the executives and board members have tremendous social and political powers. Principals expect their orders to be carried out quickly and accurately. They aren't often challenged by other employees or regulators. This lack of democratic process and accountability makes them more susceptible to support authoritarian regimes. Democracy is viewed as a threat that could lead to unprofitability and bankruptcy. Democracy is an obstacle to their own rule and decision-making process. If they can subvert the regulatory and oversight process, they will.

If the corporate community inculcate into a culture where they can easily interfere in the legislative process, and expect to defeat industrial regulation and taxes, it sets them up for more disappointment if laws are suddenly passed that disrupt their authority and profits. They will have less faith in democracy itself and soon start organizing resistance to the legislative and electoral processes. Disappointment breeds discontent and they will actively pursue austerity policies than can destabilize the democracy. They will support candidates that are easily corruptible and share profit incentives. They will have lawyers on retainer and teams of lobbyists to interfere in the legislative process. More importantly, they will support parties threatening default and government shutdowns. If the democratic government is forcibly shutdown for an extended period of time, the corporations become the largest, most capitalized, and most capable organizations in the nation. Any previous inhibitions will be lost, and they can organize with impunity. They stand to gain the most in the vacuum of power, and will easily be able to choose the next form of government.

4 BOUNDARIES OF LOYALTY

Nations are defined more by their government type than territorial boundaries. A nation that regulates itself and taxes itself is under a democratic process is more ordered state than a totalitarian regime. Its elections reflect the interests of its citizens. Its public policy is responsive and adaptive to their concerns. Democracy is more than a process; it defines the character of the nation. The United States is in a remarkable position of only ever existing as a democracy. Prior to its incorporation of a nation, it was a group of colonies with limited rights and no sovereignty. As a nation, the United States has not had known any other government type. It has always been a democracy and hopefully will always be. Few states share this distinction. In the new environments of debt default and government shutdowns, where secession is likely, political parties must not risk or sacrifice democracy to protect their territorial boundaries. A democracy ceases to be the same nation if it yields to authoritarianism. However, the same nation may add states or subtract states without making a material change to the substance of its character or identity.

The loss of democracy is far more serious than the loss of territory. Not only could it be permanent, but any effort to resolve the situation is likely to result in loss of states, regardless of the effort. Authoritarianism only delays the risk.

Eventually the people will rise to overthrow the illegitimate government, and when that day comes, there will likely permanent changes to the territorial boundaries of the nation. This delay comes at a steep cost, with loss of civil liberties and voting rights, and the inability to lodge an institutional protest. States must immediately organize resistance to authoritarianism even if it risks splitting the nation in two. The chances of recovering the states and restoring their rights is higher if a large number of states retain their autonomy and preserve democracy after the conflict. They can act from the outside, using trade incentives, aid, and international pressure to lobby for the liberation of the occupied and despotic states.

The modern era is more unforgiving than prior periods. The ability for a contemporary government to apply surveillance and disrupt resistance movement is certainly more improved. Other periods allowed the public to meet discretely to plan and organize. Pamphlets and speech were more anonymous. Facial recognition technologies could terrorize a population into non-participation. Poor union membership and labor rights increase the risk for protesters, if they can be fired more easily after being recognized or arrested. Social Media can be a productive piece of resistance movements but it is easily tracked and recorded for use as evidence. It is much easier to vote for candidates who are lawfully entitled to shut down a government and lodge an institutional protest. People are already organized into cities and states and we must leverage that advantage to coerce peaceful regime change and protect our democratic entitlements. It only gets harder after authoritarianism roots itself in the electoral process, due process, and public policy.

Optimizing solutions to protect territorial boundaries and preserve high quality democracy is only possible with informed and engaged electorate. It is the only way a minority party or opposition party can impact the outcome of a crisis while not holding/ the executive office. The circumstances should be priced into all elections prior to an event, with expectations of holding their representatives accountable during future elections. This isn't possible if the public is uninformed or misinformed. The element of surprise and sense of urgency will cause a larger proportion of the public to make worse decisions. They will either be overly risk adverse or they will disregard all of the possible consequence. If all of the possible outcomes are considered prior to an event, the public will moderate their expectations and change their policy preferences. If the politicians then contradict the preference of the people, they are more likely to lose the next election or face incarceration for embarking on a dangerous misadventure like secession.

Full information dissemination improves the outcomes in most scenarios. Optimizing outcomes without an informed electorate is impossible in the most likely outcomes and the worst-case scenarios. Optimized outcomes can't be realized with optimized expectations. They can only be realized with good inputs. Inputs equal output and if there are unrealistic expectations, the preparation and effort will be lacking, producing suboptimal outcomes. This is where tradeoffs are made between preserving democracy and protecting the territoriality integrity. If one expects only average outcomes, then it is very likely that either the quality of democracy is degraded or some of the states are lost to authoritarianism. If the quality of democracy is degraded too much, then all of the states could be lost to authoritarianism and a worst-case scenario is acquired.

Any state in open rebellion benefits from a cause supported by larger sample sizes with more accuracy and certainty, but only those states declaring support for democracy can claim legitimacy. Although the residents seeking secession may have numerical superiority and satisfy thresholds for both accuracy and certainty, they are intended to deny the minority population civil rights and voting rights and this invalidates their claims. Any political act that removes the ability of a future population to invalidate that claim, is invalid itself. A singular act must be able to be cured at a future date, if the sympathies of the same population change their preferences for the previously supported policy position.

A state that secedes but remains democratic, always has the opportunity to support future reunification. A state that successfully secedes, but disenfranchises its population of voting rights, ceases to have legitimate authority to take that action. The minority populations in a democratic state preserve their most important rights and protections, reducing the severity of separation from the larger union. The minority populations in a despotic state suffer the greatest loss in economic rights and civil rights with no guarantee of ever regaining them. Any cities or states seceding from a despotic nation, always have implicit authority and legitimacy if they seek democratic rights during the act for the same reasons. However, legitimacy and authority are not equated with capacity and any adventure may end with a severe reduction in rights or privileges, on a temporary basis for democracies and a more permanent basis for authoritarian regimes.

Sample sizes increase as the state population increases. The larger the populations the more they will consider all perspectives and possible outcomes. This is why individuals can't assume responsibility for the city or state and only the group can assert the right to organize into an institutional protest. The electorate must be educated on the issues, the risks, the benefits, and the probability for success. If there are any informational asymmetries, it could skew the decision and result in poor performance or poor outcomes. When a number of states with populations the size of New Jersey, New York, Illinois, and California all have similar election outcomes on the issues of separation or secession, it reduces the odds of making a mistake in assumptions or evaluations of the risks and consequences. An institutional protest is intended to accommodate the slow deliberative but adversarial process of disentangling democratic states from authoritarian states by way of informed elections and public policy.

The argument that individuals are empowered to openly discuss institutional protests for use in peaceably coercing regime change is based in the fact individuals have no personal capacity to implement the strategy, and if it were acted on by elected officials, it would be with the full authority of the electorate and the upper house of a legislature. There should be no doubt that when the citizenry organizes to protest outcomes of an election deemed illegitimate, they should be fully supported by their representatives with a prolonged government shutdown. Independently, neither individuals nor their legislators have the explicit authority to permanently shut down the government, but when acting together, they hold inalienable rights to protect themselves with an institutional protest. Legislators can act alone, as they have implicit support of the electorate, but it is a weaker position. This is why valid elections are critical. They shutdown will only last as long as they wait until the next election. If the public supports their legislators, they government shutdowns can continue indefinitely until the executive resigns or is replaced during a subsequent election.

Sampling size reduces the likelihood of error. This empowers states to take actions on institutional protests. Although, the probability of error is minimized, the magnitude or severity remains unchanged. An institutional protest may be an inappropriate response but at least the consequences have been considered. At very least there is a discrete number of people accountable to the electoral process who were responsible for the event. It should be noted, institutional protests are only appropriate under certain circumstances. They may always be legal but they are only legitimate when used to intervene in a corrupted or compromised election. They are only appropriate when used to prevent anti-democratic polices from further compromising the electoral process and curtailing civil rights. Most other circumstances can be accommodated by winning elections and passing laws.

All institutional protests are in the eye of the beholder. These decisions and interpretations rely mostly on discretion. The administration will assert the authority to act despite the protest of the legislature, and see any state level indictments as an overt act of rebellion. Most governments act under emergency powers to suppress rebellions and a significant portion of the population will assert the government's right to circumvent the government shutdown. This is especially true when it is expected that future elections will change the disposition of the legislature and end the institutional protest. If the obstruction in appropriations is temporary, there is every expectation the government will be reconstituted, validating their continued operations despite the interim shutdown. It is expected that in highly charged partisan political environments constituents will steadfastly support those organizations and parties they identify more with, regardless of the position or offices occupied.

Just because an institutional protest is inappropriate doesn't mean it won't be pursued. If these protests are lawful and accessible through due process, there will be political parties and individuals who abuse the procedures. Certain political parties will want to preserve power during demographic shifts. Others will want to preserve power during periods of wealth inequality. There are virtually no other limits on the use of institutional protests outside of intervention by the electorate to remove the advocates from office before the act is performed. As damaging and unpredictable as they are, presidential democracies need the possibility of institutional protests to protect against authoritarians. The people need to be able to discourage the bad behavior. However, all good laws can be abused by bad people and bad parties. It's an exploitation that has occurred throughout all of history and it will continue in the foreseeable future.

Neither the federal government nor the state governments will be acting legally or constitutionally, which reduces all justifications for the behaviors to discretion. If both are in the wrong, citizens are free to choose who to support. it is a wrong decision regardless of the position expressed. This is a fundamental aspect of all crises and conflicts, and which ever group can support their conclusions with revenues and labor will eventually win out. This will pass the priority to states, which collect the taxes and are more proximate in residency. All of the state's revenues collections, personnel management, and appropriations will remain unchallenged placing them in a superior position. The more the electorate relies on discretion the more likely one party deems elections invalid. Once a leader's behavior is determined to be illegitimate and its elections invalid, the nation suffers the greatest risk of permanent separation.

A light source doesn't throw a shadow. Most governments correctly asses the risk in foreign policy but there is a strong unwillingness to consider the threat from the majority-demographic group. This is because they are neighbors, coworkers, family, and friends, at one point or another. However, unless challenged with an institutional protest, they won't interpret their own party's actions as villainous or dangerous without having to resort to violence to protect those outcomes. If the opposition party doesn't resist, the constituents wont object to the majority party's pursuit of anti-democratic policies. Even if violence is used, only a portion of the majority party's constituents will reconsider their part. Many will see the violence as a defense of the nation and their social, political, and economic positions.

The opposition party must quickly evaluate their position and organize an institutional protest to limit the authoritarian's ability to pass laws that may extend their term or install illegitimate legislators and governors. If legislators view the current administration as a threat, they can shut the government down. An institutional protest can last until the next presidential election is held, prematurely ending a president's effective term. It is a risky maneuver and success isn't guaranteed, but if they truly fear an authoritarian pursuing anti-democratic policies, they will be forced to act in this manner. If the opposition party preserves at least one majority in just one of legislative chambers, they can keep the federal government shutdown until the end of the Presidents first full term in office. With borrowing authority and appropriations exhausted in the first few months of the president's first term, the protesting states can wait out the remainder of the president's term without fear of reprisals or other authoritarian interventions.

If the opposition party waits too long, they run the risk of losing a majority in at least one legislative chamber, and losing the authority and capacity to force an institutional protest. The authoritarian could invalidate elections or start arresting members of the activist party. Not only would this neutralize their most vocal opponents but it may subdue the electorate. If the opposition party hesitates, they could lose away their only opportunity they have to prevent a decline of the nation into despotism. The opposition parties should have more confidence during these situations. There is no guarantee that the party shutting down the government loses the next election cycle, which means a federal government could effectively be shut down for an entire presidential term. Four or six years could mean the difference between life and death for the opposition party and their constituents.

These are new rules. Most rebellions don't occur with institutional support. They occur outside the bounds of the law. They are secretive and illegal. Institutional protests are different. When states are involved, due process is weaponized and supported by aggerates in labor and capital. States are more inhibited and more responsible than individuals. They ae more legitimate actors during rebellions. They act more openly and can be held accountable for their decisions. Institutional protests are far less frequent but will be more effective. Lower order and more spontaneous mob-styled rebellions are typically unlawful and much less effective. Generally, individuals don't have the judgement or the authority to embark in revolt. They are prone to more violence and there are worse outcomes when they are successful. When political parties and states are protesting, the probability of preserving democracy will improving. There are definitely far fewer examples to draw on in history but these acts would set precedent for other rebellions in flawed democracies.

Non-violent protests are more effective than violent ones. One reason, is that they can be planned in advance with little fear of prosecution. If government shutdowns are part of the legal process, it will be necessary to examine the outcomes and plan strategies that will make the institutional protest more effective. The behavior is lawful and incentivized. It is also the purview of the state and not an action any individual can pursue by themselves. This will impart some legitimacy to the protest while supporting it with more resources than any individual can provide. More importantly, the state can act openly in their emergency preparation planning with real applications to plausible situations. Individuals attempting to subvert the government will ordinarily have to act secretly with less information and always fearing prosecution. The openness of the states planning will also work to discourage bad actors within other states or the federal tier, and avoid a situation where an institutional protest may be needed.

The fog of war is not only on the battlefield. Uncertainty follows all who might act to resist authoritarianism. Behaviors that might otherwise not elicit sanctions under a democratic regime may be criminalized under a future regime, adding an air of danger to ordinary conversations or actions. A government doesn't have to take any overt action, they merely have to threaten retaliation for the behavior. This chilling effect will harm the quality of journalism and alter the social networks of citizens. Those people who do not tolerate risk will ostracize those that speak up or demonstrate. People can be fired from their jobs, they can lose their best friends, or be incarcerated for peaceably protesting. When civilians do act out and demonstrate, they will be arrested and serve as reminders of which belief systems will be tolerated by the authorities.

In order for the citizenry to react to authoritarianism before it roots, individuals must accept the possibility of poor outcomes from behaviors that were previously condoned but now are criminalized. This tolerance for risk is not common. Most citizens are risk averse. They have children, careers, and families to protect. They do a simple cost benefit analysis and determine they would survive a totalitarian regime, maybe thrive, so, they don't act. Another group of citizens will recognize the threat and immediately react to the deteriorating conditions They say what needs to be said. These individuals all perform a cost benefit analysis were their voting rights and civil rights are more highly valued than their jobs, friends, and the loss of their freedom. They organize into peaceful protests and demand reform. They mobilize themselves and their communities for more competitive elections. Most individuals don't have the necessary judgement and inhibitions to navigate these situations successfully.

Individuals take on most of the risks when democracy is threatened, but the states are much more effective adversaries of authoritarians. States have the necessary sovereignty to defend their rights and responsibilities. When the states mobilize to protect themselves against authoritarians, they demonstrate leadership. A demonstration of leadership accomplishes two goals. The first, it reduces the stress on individuals to act, eliminating individual acts of violence or terrorism. An increased fear of loss produces an increases risk of bad behavior. Bad behavior is any individual or group pursuing violence towards another group or institution. These acts of terrorism can hamstring a valid institutional protest or popular movement intended to protect against authoritarianism. Terrorism pass priority and authority back to the authoritarian government. A larger portion of the public will fear social groups and states associated with the goals of unlawful terrorist organization.

The second, it implies protection for those citizens organizing protest and speech to defend themselves. When the state makes declarations, it emboldens more of the population to stand with the state, increasing future enlistment, and creating the opportunity for unknown solutions to present themselves. The most effective response is through collective bargaining, and states offer individuals a legal and safer way to protect their economic rights and voting rights. The public will feel more secure with an activist government supporting them. If the terrorists ally themselves with the authoritarian government it passes priority and authority to the democratic government. The state will have more support in passing laws that marginalize and mitigate supporters of the authoritarian regime.

Individuals don't have the judgement necessary to take any other option besides protest or boycott. Individuals don't aren't accountable to the electorate either. This makes them more culpable and they can certainly be arrested. Institutional protests give individuals who would otherwise resist with inappropriate behavior, the outlet to organize and act in a coordinated manner. Institutional protests occur over weeks and months with plenty of opportunity for debate and discussion. This should collar the animal spirit that deforms groups into mob rule. It's safer for the individual because they can avoid arrests and they don't have to commit to individual acts. They can defer to the group and work to peaceably achieve their goals of regime change or reform.

Individuals don't have the judgement to participate in similar acts. They don't have the wisdom and the perspectives an electorate has. The states benefit from the wisdom of a crowd and are superior to an individual's guess or approximation of conditions. An individual, not elected to office, isn't vested with the responsibility to make decisions for an electorate. This makes institutional protests acted on by states and parties far more effective and legitimate than those protests and rebellions initiated by individuals. Individual protests are rarely successful with a high risk of being condemned by the electorate. Individuals have no rights to refuse to pay taxes, or prevent agencies from conducting business, but their elected officials do.

When absolutely necessary, the states must mobilize their militias to ensure the public has the opportunity to publicly protest the loss of voting rights or civil rights. The state police and national guards will protect against abuses by federal laws enforcement or local law enforcement which may be too eager to engage and oppress the public. Calling up the militia is the best protection against an ambitious authoritarian trying to consolidate power after a compromised election. It is a declaration that democracy is non-negotiable and concessions will not be made that result in a deterioration of voting rights or civil rights.

Preventing authoritarianism requires quick action. States have to weigh the fear of authoritarianism versus the loss of political allies in the states supporting the despot. This is the hardest choice to make but it often made by necessity. If the nation succumbs to despotism without an institutional protest by the democrats, then the party won't be in a position to help any of their constituents. They will all share the same fate with little recourse or hope in challenging the authoritarian. However, if a group of breakaway state gain independence and retain the democratic entitlements, they can more effective defend the civil rights and economic interests of the minority poultice trapped in the authoritarian states. The democratic states can use financial incentives to protect the rights of their political allies. They can use international institutions to lobby and intervene on their behalf. More importantly, the democratic states can martial their capital and martial resources to intervene if necessary. All of these strategies are inaccessible if they remain part of the distressed political union.

Demographic shifts present different political outcomes than ordinary environments. During periods of wealth inequality, homogenous populations will vote for reforms while in heterogenous populations they will vote on issues of racial identity and neglect inequality. Inaction causes the wealth inequality to exacerbate, and the majority demographic will blame minorities and immigrants for the deteriorating conditions. The animus that would normally be resolved by wealth transfers, antitrust regulations, and policies aimed at remediating poverty is transformed into a miasma of mass incarceration targeting minorities and immigrants and industrial deregulation. When a homogenous population is present, the political markets act rationally, but when there are large minority and immigrant populations the majority demographic seeks to preserve the culture and institutions that created the wealth inequality. This erodes the quality of the democratic institutions providing oversight and accountability in elected officials. he wealth inequality and corruption will abrades the confidence and trust citizens have in institutions and the government. This creates an environment where a significantly larger portion of the population will be susceptible to radicalization and authoritarianism.

A nation may overcome an earlier period of wealth inequality by passing labor reforms, progressive taxes, and anti-trust acts but this is no guarantee the nation overcomes another bout of inequality and corruption. A larger portion of the demographic-majority will vote on identity politics and obstruct any attempt to reform the wealth inequality. This increases the systemic risk of authoritarianism, when the poorer segments of the majority demographic group lose confidence in the government as the economic conditions for them deteriorate. They will experience higher rates of unemployment, with lower wages, and less class mobility but have no clear pathway to change the system contributing to their poverty.

They won't identify with the reform party and refuse to support those economic policies that may raise wages, distribute welfare, and grant access to healthcare or education. These voters will be in crisis with no apparent recourse. This may incite them to violence or to organize with separatist or white nationalist groups. The political party favoring the majority demographic group will be pursuing public policy that preserves their political power though policies of partisan redistricting, deregulated campaign finance, and voter suppression. The rapid deterioration of the public sector will reinforce the anti-government or white supremacist tendencies in the population.

Debt default and government shutdowns are an irrational response to debt accumulation. Ulterior motives centered around the loss of political power and majority demographic status, are far more likely to be the source of the incentives for debt defaults and government shutdowns. Spending is a product of the electoral process. In normal environments, parties will be more interested in winning election and making the policy decisions to limit spending and repay debt. When there is an expected loss of majority political power, the party will cease relying on electoral outcomes, and start threatening violence to achieve the same goals. These parties have already assessed the risks of default or secession, and prefer them to losing future elections. The outcomes may even be considered equivalent, which then justifies the support of authoritarians to limit the risks of electoral losses.

The response is irrational because the party claims the only way to protect the nation from excess debts is to use those debts to destroy the nation. The irrationality is a symptom of the intervention advocated for. The parties supporting incremental tax reform and budget cuts as solutions implicitly take into account the long-term outcomes. The parties threatening default only see the short-term welfare of the nation because the intervention sought abruptly terminates the sovereignty of the nation. It factors in the worst possible outcomes in the short term and then punctuates it by the premature end to the nation. It is similar to how the poor outcomes and judgement associated with suicide may artificially create the urgency and poor outcomes used to justify the act.

It's backwards. It's also illusionary. If the party or person automatically rules out suicide, then they focus on long term actions that can improve the expected outcomes. Nations are no different. Parties that aren't ideologically opposed to raising taxes will see it as the natural way to pay off debts. Sovereign debts are also mitigated by inflation and GDP growth making patience of if the best methods to overcome high debt to GDP ratios. If the government maintains a balanced budget for 20-30 years (on average), inflation and GDP growth will act to devalue the debt on the balance sheet and dissipate the threat. Debt isn't optimal but it does not pose an immediate risk to the sovereignty of the nation.

The motivations for the party making the threats can then be diagnosed as fear of losing political power. An artificial parameter is placed on the expectations of a majority demographic group when that group loses majority status and majority political power. This is the same mechanism suicide presents in individuals. Suicide makes it impossible a person acquires the future outcomes to prove the strategy irrational. The abrupt end forces the individual to emphasis the most immediate history rather than pricing in a future with improved outcomes. The suicidal ideations create urgency when the poor history is punctuated with a premature end, artificially justifying its use. Debt defaults and prolonged government shutdowns simulate suicide for states rather than individuals. The majority-demographic group is basing their expectation of collapse, not on the ability of the government to pay its debts, but on their future support of a government where they are expected to be oppressed minorities. Everybody should beware the consequences of these assumptions.

The waning political party is basing their expectation of loss in sovereignty on their own actions while they have majority power. This is insider information and should be weighted more heavily than the minority party's expectations. The demographic majority party still has the political power to act on their threats while the minority party has few options to defend themselves. The emergent demographic group over-estimates the likelihood of addressing the debt issues, because they under-state the risk the waning demographic party poses. It is wiser to take the parties on their word and predict conflict in the near future. In the same respect the majority-demographic party over-emphasizes the abrupt end to sovereignty, the minority party refuses to accept it as possible. This is also an irrational position based on unreasonable expectations.

When threats of default and government shutdowns are present, it is evidence enough that the waning demographic group has weighed their alternatives and won't rule out a scorched earth approach to maintaining power. It does not matter if the majority of their constituents would support this type of action. This is the other most common estimating error an opposition party makes. Most political decisions are made without the implicit consent of the majority of citizens. The legislators can act on a default or prolonged shutdown unilaterally, without any debate or consideration preceding the event. Republican governments give legislators the authority to act on their own judgement without the need to seek prior approval. This presents another problem. Their constituents are more likely to continue supporting their political party after an event, especially in an adversarial environment with talk of dissolution or secession. Support is likely to increase during a crisis because the risk is greater. Thus, the opposition party cannot count on a rebuke of the party causing the default or shutdown.

A debt default can happen without much of a warning, especially if the opportunity presents itself annually and everybody has inculcated into the culture of regular budget showdowns and possible defaults. The opposition party is fooling itself when they believe that the other party won't act on their threats. They only have two options. They must immediately reciprocate threats and time an event to maximize their chances at preserving the union. Or they must, move their response off the federal balance sheet and develop emergency responses on the state level. State level response will be much more effective, given the propensity for shutdowns to completely disrupt and federal governments ability to intervene in case of secession.

There are other fates worse than an immediate and abrupt challenge to the authority of a democratic government. Perpetuating an environment of default threats and government shutdowns is a win-win situation for the waning demographic-majority group when they can paralyze the regulatory system and public finance system with legislative obstruction and constant threats of default or shutdown. They will preserve a weakened government that can't enforce laws or tax the ever-increasing wealth of federal corporations. They will also preserve the culture of crisis where they can abruptly end the nation with a permanent shutdown or peaceful dissolution after default. In this respect, the reoccurring threat of default or shutdown are hyper-rational from a party that has distinct incentives and expectations from the opposition party.

5 RESISTING AUTHORITARIANISM

Frogs boiling in water often dont respond to the incremental increase in temperature until it is too late. Voters in lower quality or flawed democracies have the same tendencies. Slowly, the older democracies acquire representational deficiencies like partisan redistricting, deregulated campaign finance, Voter ID laws, and other voter suppression tactics. Like frogs, the citizens may not be aware of how dangerous the situation is. They will rely on old data to make decisions and risk assessments. They will overemphasize the monuments and speeches of prior eras, without taking into consideration the new context and conditions. If the parties dont respond with public policy and pressure to reform, the public's expectations will continue to sink. It is when conditions completely deteriorate, the prospect of a secession or dissolution becomes justified.

It is backwards. A lack of education and effort prior to the conflict makes it more likely to occur, rather than less. It is pure superstition to believe the parties can improve the odds of navigating a demographic shift or other obstacles by keeping information and arguments away from the public. Without awareness, there is scant possibility of change. Without change, the nation will falter. When nations falter, they risk authoritarianism or occupation. Adapting to change is a constant. This is true for all biological organisms. Nations and states are no different. They must continue to evolve or face extinction. If we dont change, we won't pass on our principles, innovations, and culture to the next generation.

When an authoritarian threatens due process with anti-democratic policies, it may mobilize the public to protest. Protesters will try and force the president to resign and the larger the number of activists, the more likely this outcome is. Protesters are highly visible agents of change. Protesting is a public demonstration of disapproval and the president's own party may seek to limit their exposure to election losses by coercing a resignation. Protesters tend to be more successful when they acquire at least 3.5% support[2]. It is considered the golden rule for regime change and reform. Protests that exceed this threshold are much more likely to win concessions while protests that miss this threshold have diminished chances for regime change or reform.

All protests exceeding the 3.5% threshold should be supported by government shutdowns. A government shutdown will ratchet up the pressure on the president to reign. Not only will the executive be vilified by public but most of the agencies and departments of the government will be on furlough. This lowers the risks of violence or arrest for protesters and embolden supporters. If the protests don't already exceed 3.5%, a government shutdown will push the number of protesters passed the threshold and win reform or recall[3]. The government shutdown opens up other possible paths to regime change. If the president oversteps any boundaries or authority, the opposition party can then respond with impeachment proceedings. The president will be blamed for both the protesters and the shutdown, increasing the odds of regime change prior to the next election.

Institutional protest is intended to give public opportunity to organize a more effective protest and force a

---

[2] Darian Woods, "The Magic Number Behind Protests", accessed on 9/10/2019, retrieved from https://www.npr.org/ sections/money/2019/06/25/735536434/the-magic-number-behind-protests
[3] Darian Woods, "The Magic Number Behind Protests", accessed on 9/10/2019, retrieved from https://www.npr.org/ sections/money/2019/06/25/735536434/the-magic-number-behind-protests

regime change. If the government is shutdown, law enforcement and military won't have funding, and the administration could not use those assets to put down protesters. Peaceful resistance must be met with patience or the retaliation efforts could lead to state-level charges and impeachment proceedings. Any use of force by the administration will rally the opposition party to intervene with impeachment proceedings or state-level indictments and prosecution.

The best answer to an authoritarian's use of violence is a coordinated response by governors. Governors have the opportunity to call up the national guard (local militia) to protect protesting civilians. Once the militia are deployed, it will discourage the federal government from suppressing protesters or pursuing other anti-democratic policies. If borrowing authority is exhausted and no new revenues are coming in, the states rallying to the protection of protesters will have a better chance to organize and more adeptly challenge an authoritarian regime.

Coercing peaceful regime change is the primary goal of a government shutdown. One party can refuse to pass a budget and this can extend until the next election. There are no law compelling political parties to fund the government. Without a budget, the government can't legally fund law enforcement and military operations. Without passing a debt ceiling motion it will have no authority to borrow. It is within this period a group of states can organize resistance to an authoritarian regime. When large numbers of protesters are present, an institutional protest is reaffirmed by the possibility of maintaining majorities after the next election, despite the prolonged government shutdown.

Protesters represent the raw potential for numerical superiority and the natural authority in a democracy. Democracy is an expression of majority rule and large crowds of protesters represent an applied will. It is impossible to govern when a significant portion of the country or state is protesting. Roads are blocked, public transportation is paralyzed, and fear locks down the economy More importantly, protesters represent a current disposition of voters and future electoral outcomes. The presence of large numbers of dissenting protesters will validate the peaceful and lawful strategies involved in a state-sponsored institutional protest.

Impeachment proceeds offer an opportunity for regime change if the authoritarian does not resign. The government shutdown will present many opportunities to pursue impeachment if the president continues to deploy federal law enforcement or military despite the loss of appropriations and borrowing authority. The president will likely be provoked into overstepping the bounds when governors call up their national guards or withhold federal revenues through tax-holidays. Any federal can be used as the basis for state-level indictments and impeachment. The use of an institutional protest is a more dangerous version of snap elections for parliaments or recall elections for governors, legislators, and judges. However, it may be the only way the older more vulnerable and less efficient presidential democracies can remove an authoritarian or ineffective president.

It is brutish and less secure, but the methods may be appropriate under certain circumstances. If the opposition party fears an authoritarian consolidation of power, they will have to act fast and coordinate their actions between the federal legislature and states. They may only have one opportunity to intervene and prematurely end the administration until elections are held two years later. The opposition party can't avoid all risk. They have to weigh the risk of shutting down the government for two years or watching as an authoritarian possibly corrupt all future elections.

Winning elections during the next cycle is a necessary component of a balanced equation. Every party shutting down the government, should have the goal of winning subsequent election. They will want as much political power as possible to continue obstructing the federal government. With sound arguments, the party's constituents are likely to continue supporting the party shutting down the government. Even if impeachment proceedings aren't successfully, the prosecution will likely rally supporters to the cause of a continued shutdown. This party will still need to win over moderates and independents over remain in office, but to give up on the fiery-rhetoric of regime change prior to an event is to give up on the expectation of preserving offices during an event.

If the government's borrowing authority and appropriation powers remain intact, there is an express authority to organize and mobilize a response to an insurrection or rebellion. This limits the number of attempts and the severity to only those instances where a majority of legislators from at least one chamber in the legislature support the institutional protest. Authority in democracies always rests on the implicit support of the people and in due process. The states will want keep their representatives at the capitol, responding with oversight hearings and denying a quorum for bills. The biggest risk to an institutional protest is the segregation or invalidation of legislators from the protesting party. If they aren't present, they can't vote to continue obstructing the government and budget. If the protesting party and states withdraw from the union in secession, they won't be able to obstruct the government or suppress the budget. If the states retract their representatives, the other states will have a quorum and can more easily pass a budget and resolutions to put down the rebellion.

Impeachment isn't the only option available. If an administration continues to borrow and make appropriations despite a lawful government shutdown, the opposition party can seek recourse in the court system. They can pursue injunctions and legal remedies preventing the government from continuing to operate. This should be coordinated on both the state level and federal level, to involve as many courts as possible. This is intended to muddy the waters around a protest and give the rebel states enough time to organize their own response to the federal authorities. In most cases, presenting a viable resistance to an authoritarian over-reach will be enough to discourage the bad behavior. If the authoritarian resigns, the states can relent in their protest and re-join the union. If the opposition party fails to coerce a regime change with a government shutdown and impeachment, they can take other more provocative acts to enforce the will of the electorate and the clauses of the constitution.

Most federal governments give explicit and exclusive power over the budget to the legislature and this makes the government shutdown the most effective institutional protest possible. Any act by the federal government to circumvent the authority of the legislature makes it illegitimate and outside the bounds of the constitution. This also empowers the states to charge offenses related to these illicit acts. One of the first overt acts of rebellion by the states is to enact clear laws on criminal offenses related to agents acting on behalf of entities acting unlawfully. A federal government continuing to operate during a prolonged shutdown will qualify as an unlawful entity and all of their officers and soldiers will be subject to state-level statutes sanctioning the activity of such entities. This will expose the principals ordering interventions to criminal indictment on the state level.

Tax holidays are the second most effective peaceable protest an institution or state can participate in. It relies on due process, is nonviolent in nature and a well-organized tax holiday can completely destabilize the nation. Once the government is shutdown, the states can make it illegal to remit the corporate income and payroll taxes to the federal government. Once the behavior is criminalized, executives and corporate boards can be held accountable and threatened with long jail sentences for noncompliance. However, incarcerating the owners class is dangerous and the rebel states may want to consider using incentives rather than penalties.

More effective tax holidays focus on taxing the funds remitted to the federal government. If a company owes a tax liability to the federal government, the state can levy a prohibitively high tax on that amount to discourage taxpayers from remitting the funds. They can incentivize the same taxpayers to send those revenues to a state with a tax break. More taxpayer will rather pay the lower rates to the state than the higher rates to federal government. These strategies lack the declaration of making the act of paying federal taxes illegal, but it plays on market conditions with higher participation more likely. States will want to proceed cautiously: the federal government can impose similar taxes on state revenues in retaliation.

The state governments will have to act fast and pass laws making it illegal for agents to enforce collection laws for federal tax revenues not remitted back to the government. The states may also want to indemnify the corporations and taxpayer on the possibility of back taxes due after the government is reconstituted. This will lessen the fear of community members suffering harm as the result of the diversion. When the number of voluntary taxpayers increases, the state governments will need rely less on incarceration and other forms of coercion.

The federal government will immediately be placed on a clock, with funds quickly diminishing and no borrowing authority to extend time. Not only will they not be able to afford a long war with the rebel states but their economies will be in free fall. Revenues in the loyalist states will decline precipitously and they won't be able to support the federal government. The authoritarian administration won't be able to make up the difference in lost revenues and they will be forced to sue for peace and accept the terms of the protesting states. In the best-case scenario, the institutional protest weakens the position of the autocrat and they coerced into retirement, opening up the possibility the former union is reconstituted and full democracy is achieved.

Rebel states can retaliate against any economic sanctions enacted by the federal government with their own economic sanctions. Any bank incorporated within a rebel state will have to comport to state laws even if they have branches and services in other states. They can certainly use their leverage to counteract the sanctions placed on their leadership by the illegitimate government. Banks will have to abide by all laws passed by the states or risk having their incorporations suspended and assets assumed by the state governments. The states will have an implicit advantage if the federal government is lawfully shut down and unable to enforce its laws. Most corporations will tend to cooperate with the more proximate governments who have immediate authority over their individual branch locations.

The states should immediately the creation of regional banks that offer deposit insurance and other products normally reserved for central banks. Banks may not have access to these products and services if the central bank is shutdown along with the rest of the federal government. The most important responsibility of this new regional bank is creating new government bonds supporting the protesting states. These bonds will be backed by the government revenues of the rebel states. They are an alternative to the treasury bills offered by the defunct federal government. During the institutional protest, the federal government won't be able to cover debt obligations and this includes the federal treasuries. These regional banks will want to assume a portion of the federal bonds that are placed in default after the government shutdown. This act will restore faith in the credit of the protesting states. The states can choose which creditors are paid and in what order. They may take on a large amount of debt, but they will also have more predictable access to future revenues from borrowing.

Part of every states emergency preparedness plan will include sections on human resources with positions clearly mapped out, costs assessed, hiring authorities prepared, and financial incentives to attract disaffected or furloughed federal employees. If the federal government is shut down for two years or more, the state governments will want to be able to quickly onboard the staff they need to protect themselves during an event. The states wont only want formerly enlisted soldiers, they will want former analysts, law enforcement agents, tax -collection agents, and a whole host of other support roles. Enlistment for combat roles is often the easiest condition to satisfy with conscription. The more technical and specialized support roles take longer to fill.

Most standing armies are mostly comprised of support roles and this is where state governments can gain the biggest advantage. They only expect to act locally, so they can re-tool police training facilities, easily find barracks and housing, source food, and initial equipment. All of this can be planned out years in advance with emergency preparedness. If threats of default and government shutdown are prevalent, every state government must prepare for situations which include permanent government shutdowns or where the finances of the federal government are devastated by debt defaults and tax holidays. The tests are clearly stated and quick responses must be prepared. That is the role and responsibility of all governments.

The main objective of preparing or passing these laws are too cool the ambitions of an authoritarian. They are intended to discourage bad behavior and increase the penalties for transgressing democratic norms. If the states have a stronger and quicker response to authoritarianism, there will be fewer opportunities for authoritarians. Despots prefer when citizens don't protest and don't organize. If the people don't have high confidence in their ability to protect themselves, they remain silent and attempt to patiently wait out a term. They may even join the party and contribute to their own exploitation and oppression. If the authoritarians have less confidence in their likelihood for success, they will respect democratic institutions more. There estimates are all outcome-based. To discourage bad behavior, there must be consequences. The states offer the best opportunity to defend against an authoritarian and their capacity must be honed with theory and practice. They must have access to the public policy necessary to enforce civil rights and voting rights and protect democracy within their territorial boundaries.

A word of warning. There are no legitimate actors during an institutional protest. Any actions taken by the federal government while shutdown is unconstitutional and illegal. Any actions the states take to resist the federal government may also be illegal. Institutional protests are organizing revolution through due process, and are lawful and peaceful in nature, greatly reducing the risk of incarceration for participants. Although the federal government is shutdown, its laws may still apply. However, the federal government can't enforce the laws without appropriations and budget authority. This will be a lawless environment based on the discretion of elected leaders. There is always the threat of accountability after the prolonged government shutdown ends, but if the institutional protest results in peaceful regime change, there likely won't be any retaliation. It is also possible that the government shutdown is permanent, and there are no consequences for the tax holidays and other peaceful protests coming from the states.

In ordinary times, tax holidays are prohibited and government shutdowns are rarely used. In extraordinary times, when governments act outside the bounds of their own laws, it requires responses that also fall outside of normal expectations. The authority of the states to pursue these interventions rests in the legitimacy of their elections. Local elections are generally perceived as more valid than federal elections. Residents have more tacit control over the electoral process and it is assumed the policies passed more accurately reflect the interests of constituents. This is a significant advantage for the states during a constitutional crisis. When democracy starts to fail, the citizens will rely on local governments for leadership and protection. Most of the public policy responses to resist authoritarianism start and end on the state level.

Rebel states can increase their odds of reasserting democracy by having these laws prepared ahead of the institutional protest. If the statutes are already written, they can be presented and passed by state level legislatures in the first few days of a protest. This will clearly spell of the terms of the institutional protest and make it more effective. States should also have prepared their emergency services for quick deployment, with financing and supply chains squared off before an event. They can prepare all of the documents and polices beforehand and only act on them if the emergency actually occurs. In many cases, states have sovereignty and the certain authority to prepare for emergencies caused by debt defaults and government shutdowns. It would be extremely careless of the states not to prepare in an environment where these insults are ever-present. The better prepared the states are for this possibility, the more these threats will be discouraged.

6 INSTITUTIONAL INEQUALITIES

Taxes are the primary means of contact between the government and its people. Every income earner or property owner must pay taxes when they are due. This is not voluntary and is non-negotiable. Many people see it as coercion and feel as though all of the benefits of government go to other people. Those that pay the taxes rarely rely on welfare services and aren't often the targets of law enforcement. They feel these obligations are unnecessary and an obstacle to their own success and economic security. This promotes anti-government sentiments in the population. When politicians adopt public policy focused on austerity and low taxes, they increase the level of dissent and disdain in the public. When the government ceases to accommodate for the inherent defects of a market economy, it creates opportunities for profiteering and institutional abuses like mass incarceration and disenfranchisement. The public will start to view the government with disdain and contempt. Eventually they will adopt counter-productive or dangerous ideologies. Extremism will proliferate through the countryside and cities, threatening the nation with rebellion or revolution.

The biggest risk to a nation is a direct product of austerity measures. If the political parties continue argue for low taxes or make concessions to reduce taxes, the government will start accumulating large amounts of public debt. The debt servicing costs will crowd out the welfare, military, and law enforcement services provided by the government. Discourse will quickly be subsumed by partisan bickering over tax rates and deficits. The parties will start to rely on threats of debt defaults and government shutdowns to coerce the other party into reforms or concessions. This increases the risk of economic catastrophe from an unintended debt default. It also increases the risk of a prolonged shutdown, resulting in either a peaceful dissolution or a war of secession.

No rational actor sees a debt default as a productive outcome when negotiating for economic benefits. It would devastate the public finance system for the nation resulting in a possible recession or depression. Any engagement increases the risk of default. The very presence of threats for default indicate that the leadership of the offending party has considered secession or dissolution, and these outcomes may be ulterior motives. The public at large may not understand the consequences but the political leaders do. It is the responsibility of the opposition party to explain the dire economic and political consequences of debt defaults.

Once the culture is rooted, it may be impossible to eliminate. Debts do diminish over time through inflation and economic expansion, but these are periods expressed in decades rather than years or terms for elected officials. If the anger of the public is not discharged, it could lead to other partisan conflict over electoral outcomes and immigration. Worse, once the culture of debt defaults and shutdowns is accepted, politicians can resurrect the threats over almost any other issue. This introduces the systemic risk of default and then dissolution.

Although accessible and highly effective, it is fairly unlikely that a majority party will start a civil war by using a default. It is far more effective for them to pass anti-democratic laws eroding the quality of elections and civil liberties. Majoritarian parties can impose restricted electorates and even apartheid conditions when their government remains fully funded with borrowing intact. The majority party could then rely on the federal law enforcement and military to keep order during their transition to authoritarianism. With the façade of legitimacy, they could more easily oppress the populations protesting deteriorating conditions.

An opposition party may consider their own default to stop the progression but authoritarian governments are more likely to disregard an interruption in debt servicing and continue paying the obligations. Authoritarian government are also far less likely to be stopped by filibusters and government shutdowns. If they can still collect on tax revenues, they don't need the consent of the legislature. In fact, every challenge presented by the minority party in these conditions, may help the majority party consolidate power and rally their supporters. These institutional protests are merely punctuation marks with most of the resistance coming from the state or regional governments.

Romantics will assert that minorities and poor will be able to more aggressively and successfully negotiate for civil rights and economic concessions with threats of debt default and government shutdowns within presidential systems. This is faulty conclusion. Debt defaults or government shutdown are violent in nature and minorities and the poor stand to lose more if they destroy the organization protecting them. It is the government which protects free speech, unions, voting rights, minimum wage laws, and provides welfare.

Corporations and wealthy households forcibly deny these rights in order to maximize profits and political power. The risk is too great to threaten dissolution or bankruptcy in order to gain incremental reforms. Despots and authoritarian parties benefit more from a threat of destroying the government by either winning an important concession or disrupting the organization regulating or taxing them. It is clear that presidential systems are more susceptible to defaults and shutdowns, giving important advantages to the authoritarian parties pursuing policies like restrictive electorates, partisan redistricting, voter ID laws, wealth inequality, and austerity measures.

In most circumstances, the authoritarians are trying to preserve their political influence and wealth, thus they will see government as an adversary or rival to their own power. Authoritarians believe they will be better off without government oversight or interventions and more confident they will survive the brutal environment created by economic depression or armed conflict. Authoritarians only respect due process when it benefits them. While democrats constrain themselves to what is legal or moral, authoritarians can consider many more strategies and outcomes. This gives a huge advantage to authoritarians over a longer time line.

This is often the default position of a majority-demographic group, which superficially would have a greater chance to survive or retain majority political powers after a conflict. Minority groups are at severe disadvantages and suffer disproportionately from economic sanctions or martial violence. The authoritarians can change the demographic make-up of the electorate by pursuing more violent policies. The rate of incarceration, death, or disability will be far greater in the minority population producing an incentive for the majority demographic group to initiate violence.

The most authoritarian segment of the population is the owners class. They are the policy drivers of austerity measures, weak regulatory systems, weak democratic institutions, and exploitative labor agreements. They stand to lose the most when progressive taxes are applied to reduce the deficit or when trust busting breaks up their monopolies. Corporate boards and CEOs are also more homogenous in their ideologies and family histories. This makes them more susceptible to sectarian beliefs. They certainly share economic interests with each other and will defend them against perceived political adversaries. Corporate board members and executive officers also expect that their orders are followed. A loss in a predictable electoral outcome may more easily anger the owners and move them to activism. As leaders in their industry or fields, they may be more emboldened to take riskier positions.

Corporations often rival states and small nations in their accounting balance sheets and access to labor. They may be pivotal allies during a rebellion or occupation. They collect income taxes, sales taxes, and payroll taxes. They can withhold or redirect the revenues to a rebel government. They can do the same with military equipment, food, or other necessary supply chain products during a conflict. Their most important influence may be on voters who could be coerced to support secession or occupation through local, state, and federal elections. They are fulcrums of will that can be easily bent towards an authoritarian goal of preserving political power or wealth. Corporations are autocratic by their very nature and it is assumed a significant number of them would support a challenge to democracy, whether it came from a minority party or a majoritarian party. Above all else, they will seek to preserve the flow of revenues from weak labor laws or poor regulatory systems and profits from low taxes.

The poorer states may resist the movement towards progressive taxes but they are also the biggest recipients. Poorer states generally receive more federal tax subsidies than the wealthier states and this helps accommodate the poverty and build wealth in the states[4]. For example, in the United States nearly 57% of taxes are paid by the Democratic states while federalist subsidies are split evenly between the between the Democratic states and Republican States[5]. Republican States pay only 43% of aggregate taxes but receive nearly 50% of all federal subsidy[6]. If federal taxes represent 20% of GDP, then the Republican States earn approximately 1.4% of GDP in economic stimulus every year while the Democratic states acquire a 1.4% penalty on their product[7]. This artificially stimulates the Republican States economy when their policies may actually impede economic equality in outcomes and GDP growth. Overall GDP growth is typically just 3% in the United States so a 1.4% boost or penalty

---

[4] Department of Treasury, Internal Revenue Service Data Book 2017, retrieved from https://-www.irs.gov/pub/irs-soi/17databk.pdf

[5] Department of Treasury, Internal Revenue Service Data Book 2017, retrieved from https://-www.irs.gov/pub/irs-soi/17databk.pdf

[6] Jonathan Gruber, (2013), "Public Finance and Public Policy", page 14. Worth Publishers, New York, NY.

[7] Multiplying estimate of 20% GDP by 7% for Republican state shortfall of federal tax contributions (set at roughly 50% liability)

actually represents nearly half (50%) the total GDP growth[8]. Public policy experts may make a mistake and label the Democratic state policies as less productive than Republican state policies for GDP growth if they don't use federal subsidies as an instrumental variable to tease out the actual rate of economic growth resulting from local and regional economic policies.

The public finance disposition in the U.S. is even more tenuous when the consequences of a government shutdown or debt default are considered. The 1.4% GDP penalty will be assessed to state and municipal budgets along that axis, with those states onboarding budget shortfalls of 10-20%. In order to compensate for the budget deficits, the Republican States would have to either raise taxes or cut benefits. Raising taxes will hurt economic output, further reducing government tax revenues. It's a Hobson's choice with either strategy producing large groups of dissenting voters and residents. Borrowing may not be an option either, if there was a default on the federal budget or where an economic correction produces a drought in lending capital. It is within this chaotic moment that military and police will be used to brutally suppress minority groups, commit war crimes, impose authoritarian policies. This will be seen as an opportunity for the owners class or oligarchs to secede and regain control over the economy.

Small imbalances in federal subsidies expressed over long periods of time represent a critical flaw in the economy. These excesses often result from the exploitation of structural deficiencies in the legislature. In conventional democracies, the senate is this source of weakness. The United States Senate is the best example of this common representational deficiency. In 1776, the Founding Fathers agreed to the terms of two Senators to every state when there were far fewer states. The difference in population between the most populated states and the least populated states were far smaller

---

[8] World Bank, GDP Growth (Anual %), Accessed on 7/8/2019, retrieved from https://data.worldbank.org/indicator/NY.GDP.MKTP.KD.ZG?-locations=US

in the late 1700s than they are now[9]. There were also far fewer states that qualified as small when compared to the average state[10].

It was during the Civil War and shortly afterward where a larger number of the least populated territories gained statehood. Now, there are 50 states producing a very dangerous imbalance in representation. The less populated states are in the majority with four states (California, Texas, Florida, and New York) hosting nearly a third (30%) of the total population but only 8% of the total representation in the Senate[11]. This was never intended. The states with the least educated, poorest, and fewest residents, now greatly outnumber the more metropolitan and wealthier coastal states. The Founding Fathers would not have set the terms to so heavily favor the least populated states.

As it stands right now, nearly 60% of all Senate seats are in states affiliated with the Republican party[12]. However, only 51% of the population live in these 28 states providing the Republican party a huge representational advantage in the Senate[13]. The Senate is a necessary part of the bicameral legislative process and no laws can pass without its express consent. Even more troubling is the accelerating use of the filibuster. A filibuster requires 60 Senators to support a measure before it can be passed. The concentration of 60% of Senators in one party makes it far less likely that the minority

---

[9] Thomas Legion, Population of the Original 13 Colonies, accessed on 7/8/2019, retrieved from http://www.thomas-legion.net/population_of_the_original_-thirteen_colonies_fr-ee_slave_white_and_nonwhite.html

[10] Thomas Legion, Population of the Original 13 Colonies, accessed on 7/8/2019, retrieved from http://www.thomas-legion.net/population_of_the_original_thirteen_-colonies_fr-ee_slave_white_and_nonwhite.html

[11] U.S. Census, 2018 National and State Population Estimates, accessed on 7/9/2019, retrieved from https://www.censu-s.gov/newsroom/press-kits/2018/pop-estimates-national-state.html

[12] Anecdotal. The estimation of political affiliation isn't based exclusively on Presidential election year results but a combination of off-year, mid-term, and Presidential election years, taking into consideration gubernatorial and state legislatures election. Most states have mixed outcomes over time but they also demonstrated preferences for these parties. Other sections of the book may rely on different allocations of party affiliation.

[13] U.S. Census, 2018 National and State Population Estimates, accessed on 7/9/2019, retrieved from https://www.censu-s.gov/newsroom/press-kits/2018/pop-estimates-national-state.html

party will ever approach a filibuster proof number of Senators. These are nearly insurmountable structural disadvantages for any opposition party.

When one political party is so insulated from impeachment it erodes accountability in the institution and party. If a president isn't fearful the opposition party will be able to successfully impeach them and then prosecute them for their crimes, the executive won't moderate their own behaviors. They won't expect other principals in the executive branch moderate their behavior either, and soon the highest offices in the nation will be overrun by agents who are effectively above the law and corrupt. When the legislature does try to provide some oversight, there will be no significant consequences and this weakness will be declared. Once this culture of unaccountability is acknowledged, a culture of lawlessness will follow and the quality of institutions decline and fall into disrepair. The public will cease to trust in them and there will be no expectations of order and fairness.

Although the opposition party will occasionally win majorities in the institution, most of the legislative authority will be vested in the party with the systemic advantage in number of senators. If one party has a considerable institutional advantage in the senate, it will attract the attention of firms and corporations as an identifiable weakness to exploit. Corporations and wealthy individuals will concentrate their lobbying efforts on the political party that wins more often in those territories. In the United States, the Republicans have nearly 150% more likely seats than the Democrats and this invites a culture of corruption within the Senate. Corporations will form relationships and networks with the party and candidates from the stronger party. It's a sounder wager and more profitable arrangement.

The political party will reciprocate by favoring business practices and policies preferred by the corporate community. The Senators will use the significant imbalance in Senate representation and filibuster to prevent economic reforms, preserving the profits associated with weak labor laws, overt and rampant discrimination, regressive taxes, and exploitative wage laws. Therefore, it is a safe assumption that democracies relying on senates are more susceptible to corruption and inherently less stable. Unfortunately, this concept of a Senate has proliferated throughout contemporary democracies despite their innate deficiencies. Arbitrary forms of representation are thought of as necessary component of bicameral legislatures.

Arbitrary systems of representation are an inverse of other forms of representation. If it is paired with a demographic chamber, the senate will take on an inverse of demographic representation. If it is paired with a GDP chamber, it will take on the properties of being an inverse of econometric representation. This property runs contrary to the conventional interpretation of democracy. Democracy is premised on majority rule and popular support. The senate is an affront to these principles. Senates are aristocratic in nature. They provide poorer, more rural, and less educated states far more representation than the wealthier and more populated states, far more susceptible to the influence of firm owners and the leisure class.

A state with just 500,000 residents has 78 times as much proportional representation as a state with 39,000,000 residents[14]. It is an absurd belief that elevating the status of a state 78 times smaller than another will produce sound public policy. This is a deficiency that can be easily exploited by foreign powers or domestic usurpers. Corporations are quite possibly the biggest beneficiaries of the senate when they can focus their corruption efforts corrupting on a single institution or party. This risk is much more pronounced in nations with private campaign finance laws and weak electoral oversight.

One of the more important properties of the U.S. Senate has been lost over time. The original U.S. Constitution had governors appointing senators to the Congress. The Founding Fathers wanted other executive branches to have oversight over the federal executive and the ability to intervene if the federal executive ever overstepped their boundaries. The original check on the federal government was the governors' ability to write federal laws, oversee federal agencies, and confirm federal judges and cabinet officials. The governors have access to state militias, local police forces, regional

---

[14] U.S. Census, 2018 National and State Population Estimates, retrieved from https://www.censu-s.gov/newsroom/press-kits/2018/pop-estimates-national-state.html

budgets and are the only effective check against an illegitimate or authoritarian government. Governors can mobilize the resources necessary to check a wayward president while legislators can only debate, or shut down the government.

When the governors appointed the Senators as their representatives, they would have immediate and implicit access to the classified information legislators normally have access to. Governors would be more aware of all federal domestic surveillance programs. Governors would be aware of which National Guard Armies are sent overseas[15]. Governors would be more aware of foreign threats and responsible for ratifying all treatise. Governors would have more oversight over federal law enforcement and election laws. Governors would have quicker more informed responses to domestic threats and have more capacity to respond to them. More importantly, they could have direct influence over a chamber of legislature that has the authority to implement an institutional protest. This would coordinate the legislature with state level governors, and all of the revenues, military, and police assets they have access to. There is strength in numbers and when a group of governors thought there was enough cause to commit to an institutional protest. They have access to more information than individuals and they have more experience handling critical state security and public safety issues.

The Senate has lost most of its purpose when its representatives became popularly elected rather than appointed by governors. The federal government became insulated from outside control and less accountable to the only other executive officers who had the necessary perspective

---

[15] In 2005, The Republican administration sent a National Guard rotation to Iraq compromised exclusively of Democratic state enlisted. None of the other governors were aware of this troop deployment and the Democrats in Congress were unable to object or alert the public to the threat due to its classified status. The rotation represented nearly 20% of all Democratic National Guard Armies and should have been made of half Republican and half Democratic units. The Republicans were responding to the possibility of another compromised Presidential election in 2004, following the 2000 election when the Supreme Court intervened in the favor of George W. Bush. The information located in CRS documents was retroactively classified in 2011 and can't be cited.

and experience to evaluate their actions. The composition of the Senate changed dramatically shortly thereafter, when the states were expanded from just 13 states to the current number of 50. The entire statehood movement would have been changed if governors had retained the oversight over the federal government. Governors may have resisted the rapid expansion or at lease restricted the number, so that the least populated and poorest states didn't control 60% of the Senate seats. The more populous states would have made sure they retained more political representation in the Senate, if the Senate was more responsible to the governors.

Unfortunately, the north used statehood to win the most important battles but ultimately lost the Civil War when the majority of political power in the U.S. was assumed by a coalition of southern states and former territories. Jim Crow laws were an expression of this future outcome. They resisted integration because they correctly estimated they could in the new representational paradigm. They surrendered their arms only to embrace a Senate remade in their image. This demonstrates a important trend in politics. If the public believes their behavior can earn them more political power, they will accept conditions that earn them less representation up front with the expectation of future improvement. It is the promise of more representation in the future that will shape their public policy and electoral decisions. It will also imbue the voters with patience needed to successfully negotiate for improved civil rights, labor rights, and economic reforms. This may be an immensely powerful tool during nation building.

The arbitrary systems of representation found in most senates are dangerous implements during demographic shifts or periods of wealth inequality. Senates are a source of exploitation and instability when they are used to obstruct progressive taxes, economic reforms, and industrial regulations. Despite the terrible outcomes, most contemporary democracies still use senates to offset their demographic chambers. It need not be this way. Tax-based representation is a perfect substitute for a senate. Tax liabilities are correlated to population but not completely derivative of them. Pairing a wealth-based institution with a demographic-based institution, provides a public with an incentive to improve representation with economic growth. It also better satisfies the conditions of democracy with a representational coefficient closer to demographic than any arbitrary system currently allows.

Tax revenues directly support the government and the services it provides. Better services can be provided by more revenues. Higher revenues also produce more representation. This brings an aspect of self-determination to democracy. Those states that want more representation will make more sacrifices for the nation and work harder to increase the economic output of the state. A better funded nation will have stronger militaries, more effective law enforcement, better roads and transportation, and more research subsidies in health and technology. The investments will stimulate GDP growth and create a positive feedback loop to higher tax revenues.

Those states that refrain from over-taxing will increase GDP over the interim period and gain proportionally more political power than the state pursing shorter-term goals for gains in representation at the expense of GDP growth. These tradeoffs will help create the political culture found in the nation, and alter the traditional small state vs. large state or liberal vs. conservative divides. Political parties will have more diverse platforms dependent more on the individual circumstances of the states and the preferences of the politicians. This will promote deal making between the politicians and parties as short-term gains are traded for long term gains. These more complicated political platforms erode party control over individual politicians by reducing the effectiveness of central tenets and agendas. This will make elections more competitive across institutions and parties.

Unlike conventional wealth-based systems of representation, there is no personal benefit to paying higher taxes. Individuals don't gain more access to their politicians, or have more of an effect, than other voters. All of the positive effects of tax-based representation are expressed in aggregate terms, with the benefits for communities organized into districts or states. Wealthier states are more likely to have more districts, but each district will contain a unique electorate. Hopefully, this translates into more competitive elections with equal access among the political parties. Large portions of the electorate will associate taxes with political power and seek to maximize contributions. This will ensure the nation has the funding it needs to deliver on services for the poor and for proper law enforcement. The electorate won't resist tax rate increases when it increases their regions representation in the union or state. This makes it far more likely to avoid debt default and shutdowns in the short term.

Over the long term, tax-based representation will make sure the neediest people receive unemployment income, shelter subsides, and food subsidies enhancing their support for the government during a crisis. Tax-based representation will dramatically cut down on the number of white nationalists, separatist, or extremist sympathizers operating in the territory, prolonging the life of newly incorporated democracies. If the nation is recently formed there will a large number of veterans or radicals in the population already, and poor welfare and slow economies could incite them to disorder more quickly. The dual mandate for order always includes managing both sides of the public safety equation, welfare and enforcement, to ensure a low ratio of dissidents to police officers.

One of the biggest advantages of wealth-based systems of representation is the disposition of representation between the states can be altered by majority control over the legislature and subsequent elections. This decouples political power away from demographics. Demographic shifts result in a very slow and predictable change in political power, which may elicit violence from a political party trying to retain power despite the change in demographics. Tax laws are mutable, and thus may contribute to sounder transitions when one demographic group eclipses another in a short time span. Tax based representation can be paired with demographic representation to avert these crises while continuing to provide universal suffrage and other high-quality democratic entitlements.

Tax-based systems of representation take into consideration raw economic output but its virtues really rest with personal and community responsibility. Those taxpayers making larger commitments to the union will receive more representation. Those regions with more wealth have the capacity to earn more representation but they must agree to those terms. Likewise, regions with less economic output can negotiate for more regressive tax policies. This has a tremendous benefit to make the state more resistant to threats of default and shutdown. When the taxpayers see a direct benefit to paying taxes and it is elevated to a civic responsibility associated with voting, there will be stronger support for fully funding the government. Tax-based representation mitigates the mostly negative relationship citizens have with the nation. They won't see it exclusively as a liability. They won't regard it as a punishment.

Debt default threats and government shutdowns are the single biggest risks to democratic governments as they are the most effective means to disrupt a federal government's ability to put downs an insurrection or secession. If the federal government can't borrow any money to fund a war effort and can't pass a budget to mobilize federal law enforcement and military, it is very likely to result in a successful secession for the breakaway region. There are no other more effective ways to secure independence from a larger nation. However, if a rebel group is less likely to succeed in secession, they are less likely to bear the risks of discovery and face incarceration or execution.

Tax-based systems of representation make these threats of default far less likely and less effective. States that pay more in taxes will earn proportionally more representation and be better able to protect themselves. These states are more likely to raise taxes and reduce the number of opportunities the opposition groups have to threaten default or shutdown the government. In this tax-based system, states are incentivized to pay more taxes when their proportional representation increases to match their contribution. The states paying fewer taxes will be less able to defund the government and create the conditions where excessive deficits start to accumulate. If the confederate states can't effectively pursue austerity measures and threaten default, they won't form the culture around rebellion and revolt. With a diminished chance of success, there will be no popular support for the movement and the nation will less at risk of secession or insurrection.

This is especially true during economic corrections or other crises. In most crises, revenues will flatten while expenses increase to unsustainable levels. This won't be too disruptive to the representational disposition of the nation. Fiscal representation is based on the proportion of taxes paid by the state rather than an aggregate amount. If all tax revenues fall by 10% then the ratios of representatives between states will remain equal. This will make the response more predictable which always helps during crises. Politicians may already be frantic in their expectations of loss of property and prestige, and it would be made far worse if they thought they would immediately lose their political office. Political parties would fear the loss of political power in the event of ordinary economic cycles and the corrections that follow them. It would breed an environment of opportunism and exploitation.

Unfortunately, an uneven distribution of economic pain during recession is common. Revenues may fall by 20% in one state and only 10% in another. This can't be avoided but there are certain inherent advantages to econometric representation based on taxes. As the economic crisis worsens from one year to the next, the populations least affected will win more proportional seats in the institution while the states hurt most will lose seats with lower economic output. Although, this sounds exploitative or unfair, it will give the states with the better economic performance more political power to implement policies intended to accelerate recovery from the crises. Wealthier states have residents with better educational outcomes, better employment outcomes, more expertise, and a generally more comfortable with diversity in heredity, culture, and political ideology. This will allow the nation to overcome any populism that may otherwise result from an extended economic crisis. It is also very likely that the poorer states have worse economic outcomes for longer, giving the wealthier states an even better opportunity to pass the economic reforms and regulations needs to overcome the wealth inequality or poor business practices creating the crisis.

However, this natural advantage may discourage smaller, poorer, and more rural states from joining the political unions based on econometric representation. These states can be reassured that a census held every 10-years to smooth-out the apportionment process and avoid abrupt changes resulting from economic corrections. It is very unlikely an economic correction lasts for more than 4 years[16], allowing for the less economically developed state to recover and retain its proportional representation. If the correction lasts more than 10 years, it justifies a change in the representational disposition of the legislature that will make public policy interventions more likely. A loss in representation does not necessarily translate to a loss in federal subsidies. In fact, a recession may increase the amount of subsides as the political union attempts to compensate for the loss in GDP to limit more wide spread damage to economic production. As the regional GDP decreases, the relative size of the subsidies will increases providing more aid within the current federal framework for aid.

Most corrections will occur earlier or later than a census year and not impact the number of representatives earned by each state. Overall, the system will be fair due to the randomized timing, length, and severity of economic corrections, but all states will have an eye to regulate more effectively to avoid situations that may result in representational changes. Elections will price in the expectations of apportionment losses if policies aren't passed to correct the lack of oversight or regulation in an industry susceptible to corrections. This will contribute to a better funded and sounder regulatory environment, making the nation more durable with a more competitive economy.

Ultimately, tax-based representation provides one of the most secure paths towards durable and equitable representation. In the short-term, it over-represents the wealthier states with larger populations and more educated voters. In the long-term, it rewards those states passing sounder public policy that achieve better economic outcomes. Tax-based representation also defends nations against threats of default and government shutdowns by incentivizing higher revenues with better collections compliance. The properties of econometric representation lend itself to high-quality

---

[16] Cameron Kong, (Oct 23, 2018)," Recession is Overdue by 4.5 years. Here is how to prepare". Forbes.com, retrieved from https://www.forbes.com-/sites/-cameron-keng/2018/10/23/recession-is-overdue-by-4-5-years-heres-how-to-prepare/#5-71075324-0d8

democratic entitlements, preserving universal suffrage and the bicameral process. Tax-based representation has an opportunity to improve nation building efforts by offering an alternative to the Senate that appeals to all of the stakeholders in democracy.

7 ORGANIZATIONAL STRUCTURE

In Ancient Greece, each citizen was granted the right to vote directly on laws and public policy[17]. They took turns working as civil servants and leaders in the government. In Rome, the Senate was appointed from aristocrats and the Assemblies, comprised of elected representatives, were lesser institutions[18]. The Roman Republic introduced representative democracy. In representative democracies, citizens vote for agents to represent them rather than voting directly on issues. The democracy in the United States was a major improvement on the two earlier versions. The United states married a representative chamber with an arbitrary chamber. In arbitrary systems of representation, each state earns the same number of senators regardless of population or wealth. Arbitrary representation takes on the special property of being an inverse to any other representational system used in the government. In all of the different types of democratic government, voting right were exclusionary, usually

---

[17] Robert Longley, July 7th, 2019, Direct Democracy Pros and Cons, retrieved from https://www.th-oughtco.com/what-is-direct-democracy-3322038
[18] N.S. Gill, The Roman Republics Government, March 30th, 2019, retrieved from https://www.th-oughtco.com/the-roman-republics-government-120772

dependent on a mix of wealth requirements, citizenship, and gender.

All of these governments incorporated different aspects of aristocracy, authoritarian, and democracy in order to achieve their goals. This opens the door up for engineering new institutions based on descriptive statistics and econometrics. An institution doesn't have to be perfectly representative in order to preserve legitimacy. A nation could employ a chamber based on per capita tax liabilities, which resembles an arbitrary form of representation, but introduces slightly more variation between the more exceptional states. A nation may also decide to preserve demographic representation while splitting the electorate by tax liabilities. Other nations may elect to create an exclusionary chamber called a net-tax chamber that only admits states with positive contributions to the government revenues. These alternatives to conventional democracy all satisfy the basic requirements for representative democracy.

The first method discussed is a micro-political median partition where individual voters are separated into below median tax liability chamber and above median tax liability chamber. The second method discusses a macro-political median partition where districts or states separated into below median tax liability chambers or above median tax liability chambers. The median partition uses a median value to split a population into two equal parts, inclusive of all voters regardless of their ability to pay taxes or need to pay, providing each vote exactly one vote during each election, protecting its status as a high-quality democracy.

These two methods can utilize either national median or a state median tax liability. A national median tax liability will separate the states into different chambers while the state median tax liability will divide each state into equal parts with equal participation in both the median tax liability chambers. Each of these variations will have distinct properties, legislative outcomes, and political cultures. All of these options are considered class-based systems of representation due to the number of representatives continue to be determined by the size of the population, but each individual, district, or state is assigned to a classed chamber.

The third method discussed is a straight representational coefficient based on aggregate tax liabilities. This is a wealth-based system that assigns a number of representative districts to the states depending on the proportion of federal taxes paid. A slight variant of this method is the median tax chamber. It uses the median tax liability for the state, multiplied by the population, as the representational coefficient. Both of these version help protect the nation from threats of default and government shutdown by over-representing the states that pay more taxes, reducing the likelihood of states gaining enough support to forward those policies on the national level.

The fourth method is a tiered arbitrary system that only allocates the number of representatives to each state based on a per capita tax liability. Per capita tax liabilities produce a discreet range of representative far smaller than the straight method and is much closer to a conventional senate. The fifth and final method is a net-tax chamber that allocates representatives to only those states which make surplus federal tax contributions. States that receive more federal tax subsidies than they pay in federal taxes don't receive any representation. All of these methods rely on a single chamber and may be used in conjunction with other strategies for producing a bicameral process.

The two main types of taxes used to determine representation are income taxes and real estate taxes. In median partitions based on income taxes, the non-income earners will be included as zero entries and thus make up a moderate part of the below median chamber. In median partitions using real estate taxes, renters and other non-owners are allocated to the below median income chamber. In all instances, all eligible citizens are allocated to one of the two median chambers. Without universal suffrage, majority rule can't be determined, and the democratic system must be considered inferior.

The below median income tax liability chambers will typically be a mix of non-income earners and low-income earners. Non-income earners are a diverse demographic with retired persons, students, disabled, and the unemployed included into the group. The below median real estate tax liability chamber is comprised of non-owners and those with smaller or less expensive homes. In both cases, the below median chamber provides a wealth of different experiences and perspectives for voters and the chambers are coequal and of equivalent status or power of the above median tax liability chambers.

In a conventional median partition, there will be two coequal chambers with an equal number of representatives in each. Tax documents are used to determine which chamber individual voters belong to. Citizens who pay less than the median tax liability earn eligibility in the below median chamber while citizens who pay more than the median tax liability earn eligibility in the above median chamber. Citizens who don't pay taxes or don't submit tax documents are associated with the below median chamber. This ensures that the two electorates are of equal size and preserve the standard for "one person, one vote". Higher quality democracies generally rely on proportional representation and this is perpetuated by determining the number of representatives afforded to each state by the relative sizes of their populations. Both of these properties must be present for a democracy to be considered high quality.

When citizens are separated into separate chambers based upon their personal tax liabilities, it interjects class into political system. Those who pay less taxes generally have lower incomes, making them more dependent on union protections, labor rights, government subsidies, and welfare programs. It also makes them more susceptible to the impact of fiscal policy which may significantly lower their net or disposable incomes. They are the beneficiaries of government planning but also suffer greater hardship. These two contradictory properties make the below median tax chamber more complicated in terms of political agendas and role identity. This will shape the politics of the electorate.

The voters in the above median tax chamber will pay the vast majority of taxes and not receive many benefits. The above median electorate includes most firm owners and professionals or experts. However, this chamber also has a complicated identity. Most firm owners seek weak labor laws and lower taxes but the professionals and experts see the value and benefit in stronger labor protections and higher taxes, creating an adversarial relationship between voters in the same chamber. Hopefully, this chamber will be more likely to make concessions to the below median chamber to preserve the regular course of business.

A micro-political median partition allows for voters to change associations over a life time. Their incomes should increase as they age or meet certain milestones. Students are expected to have low incomes while graduates are expected to earn above average incomes. Working professionals will have much higher incomes than when retired. A voter can expect to vote in both the below median tax chamber and above median tax chamber during their lifetime. This will help randomize political preferences of the voters and the institutions. Not only will they acquire better role identity depending on their current economic condition, but it will make them more amenable to making concessions to those constituents during negotiations on laws coming out of the chamber.

Voter tax liabilities are assessed every year and an average is used to assign them to a particular chamber. Using an average will limit the number of times a voter switches from one chamber to the other making the association more durable. This also limits the more immediate effect tax policy has on the electorate. When changes aren't immediately expressed in the electorate, there are fewer incentives and opportunities to manipulate the tax code to gain or preserve majority control. Unlike other versions of econometric systems of representation, taxpayers can't improve their political power by raising taxes and thus will see less of a benefit in raising taxes. Both median tax chambers have the same number of representatives and an equal number of voters supporting them. The median value always separates a group into two equal parts. Regardless of how much in taxes they pay, the person will have a single vote and their state will receive a number of votes equivalent to population (or some other chosen coefficient).

There may be surprising outcomes when the nation is split by tax liabilities. The states with higher incomes tend to be more liberal while the states with lower income tend to be conservative. Liberals advocate for higher taxes and better welfare, while the conservatives pursue austerity measures and less economic regulations, creating an opportunity for coalition building. The liberals in the above median chamber can reach out to minorities suffering wage discrimination in the below median chamber. The conservatives in the above median chamber will be able to rely on strong support from the more rural, poorer, and less educated districts within the political union. Success is dependent on outreach making elections more competitive in both chambers. This will ensure that due process and debate in the political process remains robust and fertile.

The median partition empowers both classes. The below median chamber has as much influence and political power as the above median chamber. In fact, the median partition forces the two classes to interact and negotiate with each other. The below median chamber can't pass laws without the above median chamber, and vice versa. This means that either class can block laws passed by the other chamber. It forces the two classes to negotiate and agree on economic policy and tax policy.

An extremely important anti-discriminatory property is produced. If a demographic group suffers from predatory policing practices and economic discrimination, their incomes will be lower, their unemployment rates higher, and the aggregate taxes paid will be less. This will concentrate them in the below median chamber where they may consolidate their electoral power and demand better conditions. This may provide a single demographic group, or a plurality of demographic groups, a majority in the chamber. A majority can be used to embargo laws passed by the above median tax chamber until concessions are made on civil liberties, labor rights, and voting rights.

For example, if the two largest minority groups in the country were 16% and 22% of the population and they faced extreme wage discrimination resulting in 80% paying below median taxes, they would acquire majority control over the below median chamber. Together, they represent only 38% of the total population, but when concentrated in the below median chamber, they represent more than 60% of the electorate. They can use this position to demand more civil rights and economic protections. Laws require both chambers to confirm them, and this will force the above median tax chamber to meet the reform demands of the below median tax chamber before other business is conducted

When these demands are finally met and their wages increased, their tax liabilities will increase, and the minority voters will be more evenly distributed between the two chambers. After successful negotiations, the minority coalition would only represent 38% of the below median tax chamber and 38% of the above median tax chamber. Their representation in each chamber would be exactly their proportion of the total population. This adaption eliminates the fear of a constant monopolization of the political process by minorities. A micro-political partition is reactive, making it for better than conventional democracies at overcoming demographic inequities. Other democracies are more at risk from not successfully reforming their economy and preserving a condition of fear that may result in permanent exploitation or discrimination, and possibly even demographic violence.

There are other advantages in this form of econometric representation. Tax-based representation uses a median petition in most circumstances, providing an adversarial relationship between two chambers with proportional representation. This permits a nation to employ a bicameral process without relying on an arbitrary chamber or direct democracy which would introduce representational deficiencies into the legislative process. Proportional Representation is the highest quality form of democracy possible and the bicameral process makes it more deliberative and more secure.

Tax-based representation may include eligibility criteria for representatives in the below median chamber creating a fiduciary duty which can be enforced. When the representatives live in the same communities, use the same businesses, and go to the same schools, they will share more interests with their constituents and suffer many of the same economic pressures. This produces higher quality agency the representatives will be better advocates for their constituents. Nations will pass stronger labor rights, more equitable tax laws, and more effective regulation and oversight. These are the properties that make econometric systems superior to conventional democratic systems.

Representatives can be required to maintain an average tax liability equal to or less than the median tax liability, in order to continue running for office. A running average is used and if the elected official ever exceeds the median liability threshold, they can be barred from seeking re-election. This eligibility constraint will ensure those who represent the below median liability chamber have the same economic interests and experiences as their constituents. The wage paid to representatives can be set at an amount that automatically produces the maximum tax liability or at some other amount below the threshold, but the median tax threshold will apply to the entire household.

A macro-political median partition divides states or districts by above median and below median tax liabilities and allocates them to one of the two adversarial chambers. All states or districts will be ranked from highest liabilities to lowest tax liabilities, and separating them into the two groups by the median value. The use of districts will help diversify the composition of the chambers when each district is evaluated separately, and they are distributed unevenly among the two median chambers. States will be uniformly distributed between the two chambers. State-wide elections allocate all of the seats to the same classed chamber, producing more homogenous chamber dispositions,

With more accuracy in the allocation process, the states will have better role identity as either tax donor states or tax welfare states. The partition into high liability and low liability chambers will serve as a constant reminder of the institutional advantages some states have over others during debt default threats and government shutdown. This may change which platforms, policies, and measures they support. Tax welfare states that repeatedly call for austerity, despite being a primary recipient of federal subsidies, will be called out as hypocritical. Tax donor states may have more implied authority in oversight if they remind the below median chamber of the sacrifices their residents make.

The above median liability chamber will have institutional advantages when threatened with government shutdowns or debt ceiling measures. They depend less on government subsidies and therefore will be hurt less if the threat is acted on. If the threats come out of the below median liability chamber or any principle associated with the chamber, it can be immediately rebuked with a fiery description of the consequences of such an action. If the tax welfare states are more aware if their precarious position, they will seek more peaceful remedies to policy disputes. Hopefully, this will work to quiet dissent and force the parties to seek recourse through less violent policies

Macro-political systems have a lower order of organization. This may be an advantage to the nation. Each state or district has a mix of high income and low-income citizens producing competitive elections regardless of whether a straight value or a per capital value is used for ranking. Electoral outcomes are less predictable with more diverse electorates. This is in direct contrast to the micro-political systems, which rely more heavily on class distinctions and role identity. It should be safer to obfuscate the financial obligations or incentives of citizens by aggregating them into districts or states. In a macro-political partition, candidates can advocate for political policies or economic reforms without assigning blame to another party or institution. This may smooth over the wrinkles that form in class-based systems, and stoke fears of economic embargo or violence

Similar to the micro-political systems, these institutions benefit from the voters changing preferences over the course of a lifetime. Incomes may increase, education can be attained, employment status can change, while others will retire, marry, or become disabled. However, this association with institution will be dependent on where they live. This may imbue some longevity into their political affiliations and loyalties. Each party and institution will have a different culture attracting a different cross section of voters, altering the organizational strategies of the national parties, having a profound impact in leadership membership and policy preferences. More importantly, voters will develop empathy for other socioeconomic classes or demographic groups. Voters in micro-political systems have the tendency to stay in one economic class and form rigid economic beliefs with a more adversarial attitude.

The wealthier areas of the state usually pay more taxes due to progressive nature of tax laws. This will result in a much more disparate outcome in representational ratios between districts. Dividing the state into equally populous districts randomizes the distribution of representation among areas of different economic output, tending to over-represent the less population dense and poorer areas of the state. However, in states with roughly equivalent economic output the areas with larger populations tend to have higher economic output and will thus receive more representation in a tax-based system. A significant difference in representational ratios between districts in the same state will be more controversial than the slight over-representation of poorer states. When districts are determined by population rather than tax liabilities, the public will view them as more legitimate and fairer despite the wealthier states paying a disproportionate amount of the taxes.

The over-representation of wealthier states will improve the odds of the nation preserving democracy over a longer period. Nations with higher per capita incomes have been demonstrated to have more longevity than nations with lower per capita incomes[19]. As a nation increases its per capita income, it can expect to preserve the quality of democratic entitlements. By over-representing the states with higher GDP and per capita incomes, the state may be more likely to acquire faster GDP growth rates in the lower performing states. This will improve confidence in the democratic process and reinforce public policies that promote wage growth and labor rights. In time, the economic disparity between the states will even out with the help of redistributionist federal subsidies, and the representational ratios between the states will gain parity.

The most straight forward method is using aggregate tax liabilities to determine the number of representatives. Each state is allocated a proportional number of representatives

---

[19] Adam Przeworski, "Minimalist Conception of Democracy: A Defense." *Democracy's Value,* edited by Shapiro, I. and Hacker-Cordon, C. (Cambridge: Cambridge University Press, 1999), pg. 16

equal to the gross amount of federal income taxes remitted or real estate taxes collected. States that collect more taxes receive more representation than states that collect fewer taxes. Tax-based systems are more productive than other forms of wealth -based representation because the number of representatives are directly correlated to the taxes remitted to the federal government. This property has several advantages over conventional democracies with demographic or arbitrary forms of representation.

The states that receive the most representation in the federal system, provide most of its revenues. Role identity will help insulate the nation from threats of default and government shutdowns. The representatives that typically favor austerity measures and deregulation come from poorer states. They will have fewer seats. When they are in the minority there will be fewer opportunities for them to hold the nation hostage during budget negotiations and debt ceiling measures. The proportion of representatives from the wealthier states will increase, creating more opportunities to pass laws that benefit the nation and economy.

Governments that use real estate taxes as the representational coefficient will bolster state and municipal governments. State and local governments are more likely to pass higher property taxes to increase their representation, allowing them to subsidize higher quality education, emergency services, more infrastructure projects, local development projects, and stronger national guard armies. This is regardless of a party's electoral success on the federal level. However, austerity parties typically support states' rights and decentralized systems of control. They perform better on the state and local level, and when real estate taxes are used as the representational coefficient, it creates stronger states. Using real estate taxes is a concession to parties that might otherwise lose their ability to threaten of government shutdowns and debt defaults to forward their agenda on the federal level.

Governments using income taxes for a representational coefficient will benefit parties focused on deploying the federal government to check wealth inequality, protect civil rights, and maintain a strong foreign policy. Federal governments rarely use property taxes as revenue with most of the funding coming from progressive income taxes, payroll taxes, and corporate taxes. States that remit more income taxes typically vote for parties that advocate for expanding voting rolls, improving labor rights, curtailing wealth inequality, and limiting monopoly and corruption. When these states receive more proportional representation in the union, they will be able to pass economic reforms more easily and suffer fewer electoral consequences afterward.

In conventional democracies, there are significant political and social pressures favoring lower taxes and this can have a deleterious effect on a nation. The social welfare net is weaker, wealth inequality grows unchecked, deficits and debt accumulate to dangerous levels in nations that prioritize tax cuts. This erodes the public's confidence in the government and exposes it to insults over budget negotiations. Although, these tendencies will still be present in a tax-based system, the structural incentives towards higher taxes will balance them out. The states that pay fewer taxes and receive less representation may continue to prefer policies that promote lower taxes, but they will rarely be in a position to weaken the state to the point of breaking it.

The biggest risk in tax-based representation is the over burden of taxes. However, there is a natural check on this outcome too. Whenever taxes are in excess, a majority of stakeholders will rally behind tax cuts or other economic reforms to ameliorate the condition. Taxes may be adjusted to meet the expectations of constituents and stakeholders. States that pay more taxes are likely to continue paying more taxes even in lower tax environments, creating the opportunity for negotiation on the tax rates. More progressive tax rates will permit the higher GDP states to pay more taxes and receive more representation while allowing states which favor lower taxes to continue paying fewer taxes. This political tradeoff will smooth the average electoral output and legislative production of the nation, especially when the higher revenues support the projects and agenda goals of most parties.

The tiered arbitrary method uses per capita tax liabilities to determine the number of representatives allocated to each state. Unlike the senate, with a fixed and unmoving number of senators for each state, a chamber based on per capita income allows for states to increase their representational ratios through immigration or economic performance. Nation-building efforts often require concessions to states with smaller population or less economic activity, and the tiered arbitrary system is a lot fairer than a traditional arbitrary system. It is simply a better concession than a conventional arbitrary system due to the larger range of representational outcomes. States with larger populations or more economic activity do retain more representation but it is at a far smaller ratio than proportional systems. This will entice the less endowed states to participate without creating an environment where the smaller states can completely dominate the larger states in a bicameral legislature. It over-represents the smaller states by a smaller margin than most other arbitrary systems.

States that use public policy to increase tax revenues while their populations remain the same, will inevitably acquire more senators. States losing population to immigration despite maintaining the same economic output, will also see the number or representatives increase. States may pursue economic reforms that promote higher minimum wages and union protections as a means to increase tax liabilities and the number of representations apportioned to them. The incentives are there but moving the average takes considerable effort. It will be a very competitive market with all of the states trying to acquire a superior number of representatives. More representatives often result in more federalist tax subsidies, more jobs, and more investments into the state. However, they will all strive for these outcomes creating a moving average reducing the effectiveness of their efforts.

Arbitrary systems, like the U.S. Senate, contribute to majoritarian political parties and status as an illiberal democracy. Most senates use state-wide elections and this empowers the demographic majority by dramatically under-representing minorities. In state wide elections, the demographic majority will dictate the outcomes of most of the elections resulting in far fewer minority seats, resulting in public policy that promotes mass incarceration, voter suppression, deregulated campaign finance, and rampant wealth inequality. Tiered Arbitrary systems are more compatible with district elections when the state is divided into a larger number of representational territories. It is more likely that a concentrated minority population gain majority control over one of these regions. Tiered arbitrary systems don't eliminate the threat of majoritarian representation if state wide elections are used, but it does make the institution more compatible with district-wide elections. A typical senate with two senators split the state into regions where minorities are less likely to gain a majority in elections, where as a state with 4 or 5 territories are more likely to have minority-majority territories.

The last method described is the net-tax chamber. This institution only provides representation to the states with surplus federal tax contributions. These chambers will typically have terms that coincide with the executive office or another legislative office, with a determination for eligibility made the year preceding elections. All of the federal tax subsidies paid to a state are tallied and deducted from its total federal tax contributions. Every state with a positive number of gains eligibility, with the number of representatives determined by tallying the total amount of surplus federal tax contributions and dividing the chambers total number of seats into this value. Each state receives a number of representatives equal to the number of times their tax contributions can be divided by this figure. Every term, each states' eligibility is determined with the number of seats may change, imparting a measure of uncertainty into the legislative branch.

The net-tax chamber will usually be used as a triangulation chamber with authority only to confirm the laws written in other institutions. The net-tax chamber can confirm laws coming from any other institution, allowing the representatives to negotiate and make their own compromises. In many bicameral legislatures, the quality of laws suffers under filibusters or split party control. A triangulation chamber increases the frequency and improve the quality of laws passed when a split congress is excluded as a possible outcome.

The net-tax chamber can be organized around state-wide jurisdictions or districts depending on the framers of the institution. State-wide jurisdictions promote more homogenous electoral outcomes while districts provide more diversity. Districts will increase the odds of opposition parties earning representation in the chamber and ensuring that states not represented in the chamber have some allies within the chamber. States typically have homogenous outcomes for state-wide elections and more densely populated and wealthier states will monopolize the institution.

The net-tax chamber will optimize public finance by placing voluntary constraints on spending. Not all states will seek to maximize their representation but many will, making it more likely that the nation only spends on necessary programs and services to keep their budgets streamlined. The nation will run more efficiently with lower expenses and higher revenues. States will look forward to the next apportionment and adjust their spending to acquire representation, making the chamber more competitive.

The states who tailor their spending and services to receive less aid in order to maximize representation will deny their states the economic stimulus that will otherwise grow their economy. Over the long term, their economies will stagnate and suffer from lower growth rates, resulting in the likelihood they lose their surplus contributions and representation in the net-tax chamber. States which accept aid and welfare at the expense of representation will be a much better future economic position. States with stronger economic performances have sounder electorates and make better fiscal decisions. More economic stimulus will create conditions where future federal tax surpluses are more likely with fewer consequences to limiting or rejecting aid.

The net-tax chamber promotes sound fiscal policy in another respect. All debt servicing and debt repayment removes money from the federal system without allocating it to any of the participating states. This increases the likelihood states acquire positive balances as they make contribution but receive a smaller portion. Federal government will be less likely to accumulate risky amounts of debt when there are so many benefits to repayment. When excess debt is acquired after economic corrections or wars, the representational benefits to states will make it more likely it is repaid faster.

The net-tax chamber is an institution that decouples the economic benefit from representation improving the quality of decisions made. Most econometric systems favor the states with the highest tax liabilities, allowing them to repatriate the dollars in the form of subsidies and welfare programs. In a net-tax chamber, representatives will not divert funds from the federal government to their states for fear of losing their office in a subsequent reapportionment. This will allow them to perform more accurate cost benefit analysis on government programs and services. However, this may also result in states depreciating the living conditions of the lowest income earners and welfare recipients for personal gain and prestige.

The biggest risk from a net-tax chamber is the perpetual under representation of poorer states. This may breed resentment over extended periods, increasing the possibility of rebellion or secession. At the very least, it would increase the amount of dissatisfaction with the federal government and reduce trust in its institutions. This could develop into a robust anti-government culture contributing to political ideologies favoring austerity, under-taxed, and deregulated economies. These types of cultures undermine democracy in the wealthier states and put the whole union at risk of worse economic outcomes for poorer residents and diminished civil rights or voting rights.

Tax-based representation should be considered strictly superior to GDP or class-based representation due to its ability to protect against shutdowns and its ability to compensate for discrimination in the electorate. Tax-based representation is generally correlated to population size giving it the legitimacy it needs to justify support of the public and classification as high quality democracy. This is the promise of econometric representation and tax-based coefficients will deliver. Over-representing the wealthier states will encourage sounder fiscal policy and economic reforms that benefit people over firms and wealthy households. The combination makes Tax-based representation one of the more equitable and secure methods for distributing democratic entitlements.

The anti-discrimination properties make it far less likely that a demographic shift results in demographic violence. It empowers minorities with greater representation in the lower chamber when wage discrimination is present. They will be able to act on oversight and regulatory powers to protect their civil rights and voting rights when a coalition of minorities only need to exceed 26% of the population in order to acquire a majority position in the below median chamber. Minorities can rely on collective bargaining and institutional protests or powers to protect their interests and when the wage discrimination ends, so does the over-representation in the below median chamber.

These anti-discrimination properties make it ideal for nation building. If large minorities are present in the occupied nation, they are more likely to support a government which increases their odds of preventing discriminatory practices and other forms of abuse and neglect. This promise could end secession movements, rebellions, or any other insurgency that threatens fledgling democracies. The benefits to the demographic majority group can't be understated either. They get implicit political power and assume the majority of economic or financial benefits of maintaining a stable and growing economy. Econometric systems of representation increase the benefits to more of the stakeholders in an occupation government and promoting participation and patience in the newly incorporated state.

During periods of demographic shift, minority parties should already have enough political power in the lower chamber to protect their civil rights and voting rights. The presence of debate and oversight will cool tempers in an environment where violence is possible and avoid most of worst conflicts. This is not true of demographic systems where majority parties can more easily abuse minorities by denying them due process and access to military or law enforcement assets to protect themselves. Many offices in a democracy are majoritarian with state wide elections posing a significant risk of homogenous outcomes for majority demographic groups and a lack of recourse or protections for minorities.

In econometric systems different ethnicities and classes can negotiate in discrete terms of accounting gains or losses. The interval variable is income or tax liabilities, which tentatively avoids purely racial affiliations. There will be better outcomes for minorities in the econometric systems than the demographic systems. Econometric systems of representation can alter their political dispositions through public policy which is significantly safer than pegging it exclusively to birth rates and incarceration rates. This lever could divert enough momentum away from a fearful and angry majority demographic group that may be more susceptible to bouts of violence.

The language of political barter is different between demographic and econometric systems. In demographic systems, mass incarceration and murder remove the threat of loss of majority political power. The interval variable is number of persons, categorized by race. This places emphasis on racial properties of voters rather than econometrics or class. When negotiating, the classes can seek specific financial remedies in tax-based systems of representation. Accounting terms are measurable and performance can be tested in discrete terms. This allows concessions to be evaluated with more accuracy where the benefits clearly stated. Framing concessions and compromises differently will have a significant impact on the severity of conflicts. This is not possible in demographic systems where the only metrics are persons asserting voting rights, and this is the both the object and obstacle depending on perspective.

Econometric representation is intended to interject tension into the deliberation and representational process with the express intent of forcing the classes to moderate their views and come to more equitable compromises. However, this increased tension comes with the risk of increased violence. The larger number of class-based conflicts increases the odds of significant loss for one of the classes and the class may retaliate with political violence or martial violence. This potential for violence increases if there are large minority groups present in the below median chamber and they exert majority control over the chamber to embargo laws and disrupt the ordinary business of the state.

Demographic-based systems have a much slower rate of conflict but they are usually much more severe. Demographic changes are also far more predictable producing the opportunity for the current demographic majority party to pursue laws that exploit and marginalize the emergent demographic group. This is how resentment builds and how bad behavior is justified. The primary way demographic groups retain majority political power is incarcerating or murdering the minority demographic groups. In this dystopian nightmare, a majority-demographic group could use pogroms and violence to preserve majority political power and still qualify as a high-quality democracy predicated on majority rule and universal suffrage

The larger number of less intense political conflicts in econometric systems of representation will reduce the odds of a more severe violent conflict. With the increased number of conflicts comes the opportunity develop more coping mechanism and strategies for managing the stress of losing political conflicts. By ensuring a large number of less intense conflicts, it actually may make more severe and violent conflicts less likely. This may not necessarily be true for demographic systems which won't interpret winning in losing as temporary adjustments to household or firm balance sheets, but rather a winner takes all contest based on histories of abuse or fear of retaliation from abuse. The cost of losing a short-term political contest in an econometric system can be evaluated more discretely in accounted terms while losses in a demographic shift may be interpreted as more permanent and be more emotional.

8 LIABILITY SIMULATIONS

The United States is the first contemporary democracy to experience a demographic shift that will transfer implicit political power from a waning demographic majority to a new emergent demographic majority. This is precedent. This is history and all warning lights are flashing. The current demographic majority is pursuing voter suppression, partisan redistricting, and policies that make the United States more susceptible to corruption and electoral interference. They are fixated on debt default threats and government shutdowns as strategies to secure and preserve their political power. Citizens should be more concerned that our civil society and political process breaks down during a crisis.

Older democracies like the United States are far more susceptible to public finance crises than newer classes of democratic governance. There are more ways for a budget negotiation to fail in the United States. There is a presidential veto, a filibuster in the Senate, and a split Congress. There are also annual debt ceiling measures that retroactively raise the nation's borrowing authority after the country has already authorized the spending in the budget. Most years require a separate budget to be passed, and each negotiation presents an opportunity to shut down the government. Due process is not in the peoples' favor. Elections are held every two years in the

House of Representatives, and if a government shutdown occurs in the first few months of an election, the shutdown could remain in place for nearly two years until the next elections are held.

A secessionist movement would have nearly two years to organize itself into a new state, with a fully funded military, and its own set of local elections to validate the effort. In the United States, nearly 50% of its front-line combat troops come from the state National Guard Armies. These units are more easily supported by local communities even if cut off from the support structure of the larger standing army. Local police forces have numbers that rival the standing army, with many of their recruits having veteran status and access to surplus weapon systems. The seceding states would have the means and opportunity to defend themselves against loyalist attempting to preserve the union.

A few months into the prolonged government shutdown, the federal government would lose all borrowing authority, and without a passed budget it would have no appropriations authority. The hamstrung federal government could not sustain the military and the secessionist states could easily declare independence, asserting state sovereignty. Before any conflict occurs, a large portion of the armed forces would stop receiving pay and this would cause them to defect back to the states. Without continued funding, the law enforcement agencies that typically suppress rebellions, will be rendered inert and unable to investigate and enforce laws. The likelihood of the loyalists preserving the union would fall precipitously, to the point of no return, even after new elections are held two years later.

Not all government shutdowns start on the premise of independence, but they all invite the possibility of ending with rebellion. The longer a government shutdown persists, the more likely a party is to commit to secession. It introduces a moral hazard where the party shutting down the government is more likely to lose the next election, making them more likely to attempt to secede to protect themselves. Three months into a prolonged government shutdown, the party will realize the consequences and fully commit to the bid for independence. The parties regularly threatening default and shutdown have already considered the consequences or secession and are more comfortable with the outcome. It is impossible to reconcile the strategy with an ignorance to the consequences of acting on the threats of a permanent shutdown. if the demands are not met, a permanent shutdown is a likely outcome, and should be expected in more competitive political markets.

It is also an incorrect assumption that the party threatening a prolonged government shutdown will automatically lose the next election cycle. In the United States, nearly 50% of the public refuses to vote and there is no guarantee a prolonged government shutdown coerces them to vote during the next election year. One must also consider the negative impact partisan redistricting and deregulated campaign finance has on the accuracy of future elections. Lastly, one must consider the fact that the majoritarian party has nearly a 20-seat advantage in Senate, with most seats being found within safe jurisdictions for them. There is no guarantee that after a two-year government shutdown, the majoritarian party loses enough seats in the House or Senate to end the shutdown. A shutdown could easily extend beyond two years, to four or more. It is a profound political gamble to assume the same public that elected these officials in the first place, would then sanction them and remove them from office after the political event.

There is other evidence to suggest an electorate would not punish a party for shutting down the government for a prolonged period of time. The number of debt default threats and government shutdowns has increases tremendously since the 1970s, and both parties remain competitive. There has been a government shutdown or debt ceiling embargo most years since 2011 and the Republicans won a majority of state legislatures, governors offices, Senate and House elections despite for being responsible for threats of default and government shutdowns[20] [21]. It culminated in winning the

---

[20] "America's Choice 2012 Election Center", Nov 2014, CNN Politics, retrieved from http://www.cnn.com/election/2012-/results/race/governor/,

[21] "Election Central", updated 12/23/2014, Politico, retrieved from https://www.politico.com/2014-election/results/map/governor#.XSyJkPZFz85

Presidency in 2016[22] with a Republican majority in both chambers of Congress. If the electorate sanctioned debt default threats and government shutdowns, the electoral outcomes would have been dramatically different from 2012 to 2016.

If the consequences of debt defaults and government shutdowns are not expressed in electoral output unless acted on, then they may never be priced into elections. It is intuitive to assert that an electorate will respond to a debt default or permanent shutdown by voting against the offending party, but either one of these events could prevent future elections from occurring. This eliminates the chief disincentive to default or permanent shutdown. In many circumstances, it may be an incentive to default or shutdown. If the offending party expects to lose the next cycle and is suspicious of their likelihood of winning future elections, they may commit to this course of action without fearing the consequences.

When the electoral consequences are not expressed in elections prior to implementation, there is virtually no recourse for opposition parties and administrations. The Congress has exclusive authority to pass appropriations and budgets. The courts can't intervene. The executive branch can't act in any way or it will be construed as illegitimate or authoritarian. The powers are clearly dictated in the Constitution and the only check is state sovereignty. Federalism gives the states priority to respond in these situations, presenting more risk of dissolution or secession. Whenever there is the threat of default or prolonged government shutdown, most of the solutions are on the state level. It has always been a state issue and will always be a state issue, making these environments especially dangerous. There is no way to successfully predict how a large number of states will respond to a crisis. Each one will pursue its interests, to maximize its own electoral security and financial benefits, often to the exclusion of the union.

There should be no doubt that debt default threats and government shutdowns are the most effective way to successfully secede. Institutional protests be the most

---

[22] "Election 2016", Nov 2016, CNN politics, retrieved from https://www.c-nn.com/election/2016/results

significant political export from the United States in recent decades. Populism and authoritarianism are on the rise in Europe and South America, and these strategies can quickly proliferate. All that is needed now is a concrete example for the fascists to model their behavior on. The number of debt default threats and government shutdowns is increasing, along with their severity. It is a reasonable assumption that with an increased number of attempts comes an increased likelihood of an event. Every year brings a slightly different group of politicians, under different economic and political constraints, that will produce a different result. Eventually there will be a reference point to mark the decline of liberal democracies in the world.

The culture of debt defaults and government shutdown are a reoccurring and persistent threat. Any opposition party can impose a blockade on budget negotiation creating an opportunity for a successful secession. It only takes a split legislature for an opposition party to refuse to pass a budget and these embargoes can last up to two years, maybe more if they win the next cycle of elections. If there is a budget negotiation ever year, there is an almost inexhaustible number if opportunities for an opposition party to secede from the union. Holding all other variables constant, when the dominant political party threatens debt defaults and government shutdowns on an annual basis, there is a strong likelihood of an event. It must be considered a leading indicator that conflict is looming on the horizon. They have already contemplated the consequences of an event and prefer it to other outcomes.

The odds of a conflict are increased during periods of wealth inequality and demographic shift, and the United States is currently experiencing both. Nations undergoing demographic shifts are at more risk of violence or authoritarian policies. The current majority- demographic group expects to lose majority political power to an emergent demographic group, and they are responding by monopolizing both wealth and power. The demographic shift is the precipitating cause to the worst wealth inequality in the United

States since the 1920s[23]. This condition is due specifically to the abuse of filibuster procedures.

The filibuster has prevented Congress from passing progressive taxes, higher minimum wage laws, and stronger union protections that would have prevented the current wealth inequality. The legislative obstruction has caused significant annual deficits with debt quickly accumulating. This debt is being used as an excuse to embargo budgets and force government shutdowns. The number of filibusters and government shutdowns has skyrocketed since the passage of the Civil Rights Act and Voter Rights Acts. Since these two laws passed there have been more than 787 cloture votes, representing an increase of 2000% from a period of time only half as long, 1919-1969 versus 1970-2009[24]. During the last 50 years, wealth inequality has increased to its worst levels since the Gilded Age (1920s). In 1979, the United States scored a 34.6 on the Gini Index and now it is estimated to be 41, a marked increase in wealth inequality and inability to improve economic mobility [25]. There have been 21 shutdowns of varying length occurring since the 1970s, and none prior[26].

Neither filibusters nor government shutdowns were used in great numbers prior to the civil rights movement laws. Now filibusters and government shutdowns are nearly constant fixtures in political discourse. This presents strong evidence that demographic shift is the source for the debt default and government instability. There is no easy remedy. The nation can't escape this persistent threat simply by enacting progressive taxes to avoid large deficits and correct the wealth inequality. Any political success by the emergent demographic

---

[23] Alexander Eichler and Michael McAuliff, Dec 6th 2017, "Income Inequality Reached Gilded Age Levels, Congressional Report Finds", HuffPost, retrieved from https://www.huffpost.com/entry/income-inequality_n_1032632

[24] Jason Chafetz, May 2011, "The Unconstitutionality or the Filibuster". Connecticut Law Review, Vol 43, No. 4, retrieved on 2.24.2018 from https://papers.ssrn-.com/sol3/papers.cfm?-abstract_id=1730782

[25] World Bank, "GINI Index (World Bank Estimate)", retrieved from https://-data.worldbank.org/indicator/SI.POV.GINI

[26] Tom Murse, May 25th, 2019, "All 21 government shutdowns in U.S. history", retrieved from https://www.thought-co.com/government-shutdown-history-3368274

group will be viewed as a threat, provoking a response by the waning party to protect their power. At some future point, the political party expecting to lose power will assess their odds at continuing to win majorities and make the fateful decision to declaring independence wand secede.

This section examines the United States under the prism of micro-political and macro-political representation in its entirety. How would representation change in the nation, if it retained all its states and if those states based their representation on federal taxes? This is intended to offer a proof on the assumption, tax-based representation provides a strong check against parties threatening debt defaults and government shutdowns. The states that pay the most taxes also receive the most representation, making these insults less frequent and less severe. Subsequent simulations, separate the states into two equal population groups, with Democratic states in one group and Republican States in the other. The prism of micro-political representation is interposed on these nations as well, allowing one to peer into how they might be organized after a peaceful dissolution or successful secession. The states have a fairly predictable political disposition and all of the relevant demographic data and econometric data is available.

None of these models are expected to be completely predictive, given how a debt default or dissolution might negatively impact current GDP and tax revenues, or how future state legislature and governor elections might change the territorial boundaries of newly incorporated states after a secession. These events don't have to actually happen for the simulation retain their value. The axes of evaluation can be interposed on other unions or nations covering almost any scenario. The roles and positions of the states are fungible and can easily apply to other circumstances, places, and persons.

The first simulation demonstrates how tax-based representation could protect the nation from threats of debt default and government shutdowns. The representational coefficients used are aggregate tax liabilities which distribute a discrete number of seats to each state. The first property to notice is that the Democratic states would gain a total of 246 seats of 435[27]. The Republican states would have to settle for 189 seats of 435[28]. These aren't fixed outcomes and competitive elections will produce results that are much closer, but the Democratic states will have a decided advantage. The Democratic states will have access to nearly 57% of all seats which is nearly equivalent to the advantage in seats the Republicans have in the U.S. Senate[29]. Despite the Republicans having a significant structural advantage in the Senate, the Democrats are still competitive enough to win majorities.

It is expected that with 57% of the seats in the chamber, the Democrats would be more successful in passing progressive taxes and avoiding the circumstances where threats of default or government shutdowns are more justified. With higher revenues, deficits will be proportionally smaller, and they can't be used to justify the threats. Austerity policies are popular in Republican electorates, but with only 43% of the seats, they won't gain traction in the institutions and the threats won't be plausible. Progressive taxes will limit the number of opportunities that can be exploited by the opposition party, making the nation more secure and less susceptible to a premature end from insults to its public finance system.

There are other noticeable changes in representation that occur with a tax-based representational coefficient. Texas has nearly 9% of the total seats which is less than double that of New Jersey at 5%[30]. With demographic-based representational coefficient, Texas would have more than three-times the number of representatives as New jersey[31]. California has only 13% of the total number of representatives and only slightly more than twice that of New jersey[32]. California would normally have close to six-times as many representatives[33]. More telling is the comparison of New Jersey with Florida

---

[27] Table 1: Tax-based Coefficients (Democrats)
[28] Table 1: Tax-based Coefficients (Democrats)
[29] Table 1: Tax-based Coefficients (Democrats)
[30] Table 1: Tax-based Coefficients (Democrats)
[31] Table 1: Tax-based Coefficients (Democrats)
[32] Table 1: Tax-based Coefficients (Democrats)
[33] Table 1: Tax-based Coefficients (Democrats)

with nearly equal tax-based representation despite demographic-based representation favoring Florida by a margin of 3:1[34]. The states with higher standards of living and GDP pay disproportionately more taxes, and therefore earn significantly more representation. New York, California, Texas, and Florida have large populations, but lower per capita incomes, resulting in a moderate number of representatives compared to the less populated and denser states, with higher median wages, like New Jersey, Massachusetts, and Ohio.

If the reoccurring threats of debt default and government shutdowns resulted in a permanent dissolution of the Union, the disposition of representation would change within the two independent nations. In the union created by the Democratic states, California with 22%, and New York with 15%, represent 37% of all seats in the econometric chamber and 46% of the population[35]. Illinois and New Jersey earn representation at a combined 17% despite a population of only 13% the total for the new nation[36]. In the Republican confederacy, Texas and Florida acquire 32% of the total seats which nearly match the proportion of population[37]. Ohio gains the largest proportion of representation, with close to 10% of the seats and only 7% of the total population[38]. The Republican states will have lower per capita incomes and distribute their representation much more evenly. The Democratic states have a few high GDP and low population states, which makes them the biggest beneficiaries of tax-based representation.

Straight tax-based representation is often included in a bicameral legislature which predisposes the use of demographic representative coefficients or arbitrary representation. The more rural and poorer states would ordinarily object to a tax-based system of representation, but marrying it to a senate may offset the individual benefits of both chambers. It is a perfect compromise, where the poorer

---

[34] Table 1: Tax-based Coefficients (Democrats)
[35] Table 1: Tax-based Coefficients (Democrats)
[36] Table 1: Tax-based Coefficients (Democrats)
[37] Table 2: Tax-based Coefficients (Republicans)
[38] Table 2: Tax-based Coefficients (Republicans)

and more rural states occupy 60% of the senate seats while the urban and wealthier states enjoy a 57% advantage in the tax-based chamber. Elections will remain competitive enough, where both parties can gain control of either chamber in any given year, but where neither party has a permanent and systemic advantage in either chamber. During nation building efforts, administrators can approach stakeholders and offer each an opportunity they otherwise wouldn't have. Nation building requires tradeoffs, and tax-based representation provides a new tool to negotiate with. This is more important for those nations with large disparities between the population of states and diverse ethnicities and religions.

Tax-based representation is a critical advantage for rebels trying to organize a democratic state. Tax-based representation favors more populous and wealthier states, eliciting more support from the more developed parts of the country. It will attract supporters with more capital, firms with access to labor, and a diverse cross section of the public. Other econometric systems have properties that can protect the civil liberties and economic interests of minorities, making them a natural ally and reliable partner. Local and state governments, along with firms are expert at assembling tax data and economic data, which will aid credibility and support for a movement towards democracy. If these organizations mobilize, it greatly improves the chances for success. With more resources, a rebellion will have better outcomes. These expectations will increase the frequency of attempts. History reflects outcomes more than intentions, and econometric representation is specifically engineered to improve performance during these trials

Insurrection isn't the only path to democracy. Wars occur and occupying nations will often impose democracy on the temporarily subdued nation. The occupying nation may make recommendations to the newly incorporated democracy, but it will ultimately be the citizens of the new state that choose their own system of representation. Having a number of options available will improve outcomes by permitting the citizens to create a democracy that more resembles their own culture. Econometric representation provides the leadership of the occupied nation another means to organize their state into a productive democracy. They may fear the arbitrary representation of a senate in a state with sectarian rifts. They may doubt the sturdiness of demographic-representation in an environment of populism. Tax-based systems of representation offer the new nation more solutions to overcome their history of authoritarianism or aristocracy. Let them choose for themselves and let this experiment in democracy test new strategies in representation and due process.

These organizational strategies will make the democratization process more effective at all stages of consideration and implementation. Control over these concepts will permit an occupying nation an opportunity to seek out elites and organizations that will benefit from the structure. The beneficiaries of econometric representation are generally found in the wealthier and more populated states and any war or reconstruction effort will need their cooperation to be successful. At the very least, these states will offer weaker resistance to the occupation after the war is fought and lost. All firms and natural persons respond to incentives, and wealth-based representation plays on these instincts.

Democracies with higher per capita incomes typically preserve their democratic entitlements for longer periods than poorer nations[39]. Like other econometric systems of representation, tax-based systems can improve the lifespan of fledgling democracies by over-representing states with better economic outcomes. In tax-based systems, the states with higher per capita incomes receive more representatives than the states with lower per capita incomes, possibly resulting in better entitlement outcomes. When the nations per capita income is adjusted in proportion to the disposition of representation, they will have outcomes associated with wealthier states. The less developed states will have fewer representatives than the more developed states, allowing voters with better economic outcomes more of an opportunity to shape policy and laws.

Fledgling democracies also benefit from tax-based representation by providing more stability through higher tax

---

[39] Adam Przeworski, "Minimalist Conception of Democracy: A Defense." *Democracy's Value,* edited by Shapiro, I. and Hacker-Cordon, C. (Cambridge: Cambridge University Press, 1999), pg. 16

revenues and an inherent resistance to debt defaults and government shutdowns. Recently incorporated nations are more susceptible to threats of default if there is a persistent war effort or unstable economy. Citizens have less trust in due process and the candidates running for office. There are far more ways a new democracy can fail and minimizing the threat of default or budgetary conflicts will bring more certainty to the democratization process. A risk of failure is always present. When the loss of capital and labor isn't justified by a successful conversion it could discourage other democratization efforts.

Tax-based representation may increase the frequency and quality of outcomes for attempts to install democracy in previously authoritarian nations. If the high cost of war and occupation can be better justified with a higher probability of conversion to democracy, then more nations may pursue democratization efforts as a means to make their environment more secure. These two properties are synergistic. Over-representing states with higher per capita incomes creates a tendency to preserve democracy longer, while the culture of tax-based political systems will make them more resistant to premature ends due to debt defaults and government shutdowns. Improving longevity increase the success rates for revolutions and occupations resulting in national building efforts

Nation building efforts utilizing tax-based representation may contribute to sounder growth for the newly incorporated states. Fiscal policy is a major input to economic output; tax subsidies can accelerate consumption and increase profits, while high rates can limit them. Whole industries can be promoted by subsidies while others choked off from sustaining revenues. Associating political representation with fiscal policy will change the equation when it comes to economic management. More districts and states will support higher corporate taxes and progressive income taxes to produce more aggregate revenues and representation. This is very different from the current culture, where individuals try to suppress most tax liabilities for themselves and the companies they work for. The majority of persons will see a major advantage is forcing firms and wealthy households to pay higher taxes, allowing the government to take on more obligations for general welfare and law enforcement while protecting the free market economy.

With more of the most critical aspects of civil society adequately paid for the nation can stand apart from the private economy. With stronger law enforcement the nation can quash corruption and fraud. Regulators can focus on trustbusting and break up monopolies and oligopolies. When the public has free and unfettered access to healthcare, education, and other services that are easily exploited for profit, corporations can focus on more competitive and less sensitive components of the economy. The public will offer fewer complaints about the quality of economy, making them far less susceptible to extreme ideologies like communism, socialism, or totalitarian capitalism.   They will also have more confidence in the judgement of their elected officials and government. The electorate will be more moderate with sounder expectations. Fiscal representation will deliver a more capable and sounder form of democracy that will promote equitable public policy and more stable electoral system.

Other nations may prefer tax-based representation that continues to use demographics for the representational coefficient. A macro-political median partition can be easily applied to the United State in another set of simulations. Each state is allocated to one of the two bicameral chambers, with eligibility determined by the gross taxes remitted to the federal government. States are ordered by revenues, from lowest to highest, and then split into two equally sized groups. Half of the states are sent to the below median chamber and the other half are admitted to the above median chamber. This process groups states into discrete chambers, allowing some of the larger states to monopolize the seats of a chamber. There are significant implications when a coalition of just 26% of the states will acquire more than 51% of the seats in one chamber, giving them tremendously more bargaining power.

In the U.S. model, California already controls more than 24% of the seats allowing them to easily cement majority control with another partner[40]. Even in competitive elections

---

[40] Table 3: Above Median Chamber (by Population)

where an opposition party wins a third or half of the state's elections, it puts the CA delegation in a superior position to negotiate back to a majority. The Democratic states already control nearly 63% of all seats in the above median chamber giving them a clear advantage[41]. This position is significantly more important than the reciprocal advantage the Republicans earn in the above median chamber. The Republican states may control 63% of the seats but it is distributed over a much larger number of states[42].

With competitive elections, the opposition parties have an even greater chance of winning. There is a greater likelihood that deals can be struck and compromises made to get more bills to the floor for a vote. The smaller number of states with more homogenous electoral outcomes is a stronger position for the Democrats in the above median chamber. This arrangement will pull the legislature to the left, with more opportunities to pass progressive taxes, stronger regulations, and more civil rights and labor protections.

Although demographic representational coefficients are the highest standard for democratic representation, arbitrary systems like the U.S. Senate, are not only acceptable but preferable. It is thought the demographic chambers are more susceptible to populism and other animal spirits. A bicameral process that includes a senate, with longer terms and a non-proportional allocation of seats between states will be more insulated from circumstances radical movements calling for massive redistributions of wealth or political power. However, arbitrary systems can be improved by econometrics. A per capita income or per capita tax liability will achieve many of the benefits of an arbitrary system, with an added measure of variance.

Per capita values result in a range of outcomes constrained between roughly 1% and 5%[43]. Most states will acquire just 2% or 4% of the total number of representatives due to averaging out the representational coefficient[44]. In this respect, it is similar to the Senate. Each state receives a

---

[41] Table 3: Above Median Chamber (by Population)

[42] Table 4: Below Median Chamber (Democratic, by Population)

[43] Table 6: Per Capita Tax Liabilities (Democratic)

[44] Table 6: Per Capita Tax Liabilities (Democratic)

number of representatives roughly equal to each other. For example, California receives only 2% and New York receives only 3% of the total number of representatives despite being responsible for a combined 19% of the overall population[45]. New jersey acquires 4% of the total number of representatives and Delaware 5%, despite the two states only accounting for just 2% of the overall population[46]. Those states that pay more into the federal system, earn more seats in the same tiered system. The amount paid in must be significantly larger than the other states to get even a small number of more seats.

Representational coefficients based on per capita values break up the monopoly larger states might have due to population and aggregate revenues. It is the average contribution each one of their residents makes that determines their representational power. States are incentivized to generate larger incomes and pass more tax revenues along to the federal government. This benefit both the federal government and the states that pass sounder business laws. Even when states gain a disproportionate amount of political power, the amount is often more reasonable under a per capita system. In this example, Delaware is by far the most influential state but it only acquires 5% of the total vote[47]. In conventional demographic systems, states like California have more than 13%. These are the same benefits a Senate typically provides but this version of arbitrary representation has more variability.

When the nation is separated into two individual nations, the per capita representational coefficients have a similar effect. The range for the Democratic bloc is much larger with several results of 1% near the low end and several results above 7%[48]. Most of the states acquire an average of 3-4% so a result of 7% is only double that of the most likely outcome[49]. Only Delaware with 9% of the representation is a significant outlier at almost 3x the average outcomes[50]. For states that

---

[45] Table 6: Per Capita Tax Liabilities (Democratic)

[46] Table 6: Per Capita Tax Liabilities (Democratic)

[47] Table 6: Per Capita Tax Liabilities (Democratic)

[48] Table 6: Per Capita Tax Liabilities (Democratic)

[49] Table 6: Per Capita Tax Liabilities (Democratic)

[50] Table 6: Per Capita Tax Liabilities (Democratic)

object to the tyranny of a majority presented by conventional democracy, or a tyranny of the wealthy presented by most econometric democracy, the arbitrary representational coefficient, adjusted for per capita values and larger ranges, is a perfect compromise. It offers more variance than a typical arbitrary system, yet breaks up the monopoly of demographic or econometric democracy.

The Republican bloc has much more even outcomes. Their range is between 1 and 4 with most being either 3% or 4%[51]. This is a much more equitable distribution if one is trying to imitate the function of a conventional Senate. The Republicans have been the overwhelming beneficiaries of the Senate in the U.S. system, it would be interesting to see if the most populous and wealthiest states in a new Republican confederacy, the same concession to a much larger group of more rural and poorer states. If this chamber is paired with a demographic chamber, then it may be a more acceptable outcome. From the onset, the two most populous and wealthiest states in the new union will have demographic trends that will predictably move the states to majority minority where African Americans, Hispanics, Asians, and Jews have majority political power. This will complicate a decision where the Republicans chose secession over participating in a larger democracy with the same demographic trends and electoral outcomes. Maybe, the question is not what type of democracy the Republicans will accept, but rather will they continue to prefer it over authoritarianism and industrial despotism.

The next method for tax-based representation is the best for cure for older presidential democracies like the United States. Presidential democracies beset by filibusters and vetoes can overcome these hurdles by installing a net-tax chamber as a triangulation chamber. The net-tax chamber only admits those states that make surplus contributions to federal tax systems. It rewards the sacrifice made by their taxpayers with exclusive access to a third legislative chamber. When authorized, this chamber can write laws and ratify laws coming from either of the two other legislative chambers. It

---

[51] Table 7: Per Capita Tax Liabilities (Republican)

will also have oversight responsibility for the central bank, department of treasury, and similar agencies.

One party will always have majorities in at least two of the chambers allowing them to pass laws. This will accelerate the bicameral process and improve quality of legislation. The president retains veto powers limiting the legislator's authority, but this will only curtail half of the opportunities presented. It is in this respect the United States can overcome its history of legislative obstruction to pass progressive taxes and end the threat of default and government shutdowns.

There are two primary ways to organize a net-tax chamber. The first is using population for the representational coefficient after federalist tax dollars are used to determine eligibility. The second method uses the surplus federal tax contributions as a representational coefficient after eligibility is determined. Using an econometric representational coefficient allows state to determine its own political power through sounder fiscal policy and economic decisions. However, using demographic-based representational coefficient comports to a higher standard of entitlement and is more predictable from year to year if the same fiscal policy and regulatory regime persists from year to year.

The demographic coefficients produce fairly conventional results with California, New York, and Texas accounting for nearly 47% of all seats in the chamber[52]. The other 17 participating states range from just 1% to nearly 7%, but they account for only 53% of the seats[53]. The Democratic states hold 302 of the 435 seats, giving them a clear majority with slightly more than 69% of all seats in the chamber[54]. The Republicans have just 133 seats for a total of 31%, but half of them come from Texas with 67 seats or 15% of the total[55].

The Republican states have even less representation in a net-tax chamber governed by econometric coefficients. Texas and Ohio have the largest share at 8% and 9% respectively, but the remaining 6 have less than 2% each, for a total

---

[52] Table 10: Net Chamber Eligibility (Democrats)
[53] Table 10: Net Chamber Eligibility (Democrats)
[54] Table 10: Net Chamber Eligibility (Democrats)
[55] Table 11: Net Chamber Eligibility (Republicans)

proportion of just 21% of the chamber[56]. The Democrats control 79% of all seats with New York commanding 15% and New Jersey 14%. California falls to just 12% of the seats and Minnesota has an equal amount. Illinois has more than 10%, Massachusetts has almost 7%, Connecticut has nearly 4%, and Delaware occupies nearly 3% of seats[57]. The other states have only a negligible number of seats, but at least 1 per state[58].

Net-tax chambers do exclude a number of states from participation. However, when demographic coefficients are used, the chamber resembles the current Senatorial disposition. The nation continues to vest vests authority in the Senate despite 60% of the states predictably voting Republicans[59]. This is not substantially different from a chamber where 69% predictably vote Democratic[60]. There is also one very significant difference between the Senate and a net-tax chamber. States only slowly change their political preferences, while participation in the net-tax chamber can change every term. The states can determine for themselves if they want to participate next term by refusing federalist tax subsidies and by maximize federal tax revenues.

Democracy is often viewed with suspicion by minorities as it is believed that minorities are swept under the torrents of majority political will. This is the fear of a tyranny by the majority. Contemporary democracies do little to assuage this fear as most continue to rely on state-wide elections for presidents, governors, and senators. District-wide elections are often restricted to just a single chamber if the federal legislative branch. In state-wide elections even large minorities are denied representatives that resemble them in policy and ideology. It's a winner take all system and large minority groups consistently lose by large margins.

Even when the state is split 45% minority and 55% majority, a demographic majority will have monopolistic control over all electoral outcomes. If there are just two state-wide legislative offices, there is a strong possibility that they

---

[56] Table 11: Net Chamber Eligibility (Republicans)
[57] Table 10: Net Chamber Eligibility (Democrats)
[58] Table 10: Net Chamber Eligibility (Democrats)
[59] Anecdotal
[60] Table 10: Net Chamber Eligibility (Democrats)

will both be occupied by the same party. A smaller number of representatives accommodates less diversity in political ideology and economic interests. If the majority voting block consistently votes in a homogenous manner, there is virtually no opportunity for the minority party to win office. District-wide elections avoids this by giving groups of concentrated minorities an opportunity to elect representatives that align more with their interests. A larger number of representatives also allows for more perspectives and positions to be held by the politicians. When divided by districts, it is more likely that the elections will be split by party, making the overall electoral system far more competitive.

When a senate is paired with a demographic chamber in a bicameral process, it more or less puts the entire legislative chamber under the explicit control of the demographic majority. This pairing undermines the district-wide representation provided to minorities in the demographic chamber, by subjugating it to the consent of the demographic majority in the senate. The demographic chamber can't pass laws on its own and must defer to the senate for confirmation. When a senate relies on state wide elections, its officers can disregard the rights and interests of most minority groups, presenting an obstacle to the minority groups gaining any civil rights protections or protecting their economic interests. If the senate employs a filibuster, overcoming it may be near impossible resulting in a low legislative production rate and laws exclusively benefiting firm owners, the wealthy, and demographic majority.

The micropolitical median partition limits the number of state-wide elections resulting in more electoral equity being distributed to minority groups. The median partition also continues to rely on a bicameral process making it more secure than a unicameral chamber. The two chambers will often have adversarial electoral outcomes, setting them up to check each other with oversight. Each chamber will have their own culture and electorate making it very likely different parties are in office. The two chambers will have to learn to compromise on bills in the regular course of business.

The bicameral process typically entails strong partisan identities within the two median chambers, with electorates split between above median taxpayers and below median taxpayers. This role identity will help establish boundaries and moderate expectations between the two chambers and establish a competitive or adversarial relationship. This is intended to improve the quality of debate and laws coming out of the bicameral process. State-Wide elections will still dictate Governors and Presidents but at least more of the legislative authority will be vested in districts.

A micropolitical median partition based on tax liabilities also provides anti-discrimination properties. Tax liabilities are a proxy for incomes, and if there is wage discrimination or employment discrimination, it will concentrate minorities in the below median chamber. When this happens, it makes it more likely the minority group can protect their economic interests and civil rights and reverse the negative effects of discrimination. When a demographic group is concentrated in one of the two median chambers, it can effectively double their representational power. If minority groups capture just 26% of the below median income chamber, they can embargo or boycott laws coming from the above medina chamber until they earn concession on civil liberties and economic rights.

If a nation like the United States had demographics of 13% African American, 18% Hispanic, 1% Native Americans, and 2% mixed race, and if wage discrimination lowers their household incomes to 80% of the median wage is located in the below median chamber, this coalition will command a 26% share in the electorate, granting them a 51% share in the below median chamber, and majority control over the legislative process[61]. In the United States. African Americans have approximately $39,000 average income with Hispanics earning close to $47,000[62]. The median wage for the overall population was $59,000[63] where the median income for non-Hispanic whites is more than $65,000[64]. The fastest growing

---

[61] U.S. Census, Quick Facts United States, retrieved from, https://www.census.gov/quickfacts-/fact/table/US/PST045218

[62] Heather Long, Washington Post, Sept 15th, 2017, retrieved from https://www.latimes.com/-business/la-fi-african-american-income-20170915-story.html

[63] Heather Long, Washington Post, Sept 15th, 2017, retrieved from https://www.latimes.com/-business/la-fi-african-american-income-20170915-story.html

[64] Heather Long, Washington Post, Sept 15th, 2017, retrieved from https://www.latimes.com/-business/la-fi-african-american-income-20170915-story.html

demographic group found is Asian Americans, currently 5% with an average wage over $81,000[65]. It is estimable that a combination of the income properties and growth rates will produce a majority in the below median chamber, for non-white citizens within just a few years

When the coalition of minority groups effectively defends their economic interests, their wages will increase and distribute the populations more evenly across all communities, reducing the concentration of minority voters in the below median chamber. As a consequence of their success, the minority groups will lose their representational advantage. There will be less distinction between the policy preferences and economic outcomes, reducing the danger of a demographic majority's interests deviating from those of minorities. The tyranny of a demographic-majority will only persist for as long as economic opportunity and wages are fairly distributed to all demographic groups in the democracy.

During a demographic shift, the median partition will deliver a disproportionate amount of political power to the growing minority groups if discrimination is present, allowing them to protect their economic interests and civil rights a representational advantage in the below median chamber. As wages fall and wealth inequality increases, a larger portion of minorities will be concentrated in the below median chamber when they need it most. With quick legislative action, they can ameliorate the discrimination and stabilize the nation with progressive taxes, stronger labor rights, and higher wages. If legislative obstruction is unable to be overcome, then the minority populations can respond with rhetoric and debate that focuses on the voter suppression, wage exploitation, and the risk of authoritarianism. Public acceptance of the current conditions will provoke state governments and cities to develop policy responses to the threat of conflict. It will help the electorate, civil service, and political caste to mobilize in defense of the union and minority populations.

Analysts can examine all scenarios where civil society breaks down or where the federal government fails. They can

---

[65] Heather Long, Washington Post, Sept 15th, 2017, retrieved from https://www.latimes.com/-business/la-fi-african-american-income-20170915-story.html

look at the ramifications to the local economy. They can look to see how the loss of federal tax subsidies or the repatriation of those dollars might affect them. State governments can prepare laws that promote tax holidays and divert revenues away from the federal government or offending states. More importantly, the governors can start preparing their national guard Armies and coordinate with city and state police forces for an emergency response. The governors can start looking at ways to enlist large numbers of new soldiers, train them, and quickly equip them. Analysts will pour over supply chains, and look for weakness in their own organization and the other states. All of this can occur under the guise of emergency preparedness, and none of it has to be implemented unless there is conflict.

The best way to avoid conflict is to discourage it with an organized response. When legislators are more aware of the circumstances, they can prepare the public for a quick response, and ensure that state and local politicians have policies they can quickly deploy in an emergency. The risk of loss is not enough to discourage bad action. Only an organized response will reduce the likelihood of successful secession or usurpation by increasing the sanctions on individuals and organizations participating in the behavior. Due process must be protected and a fully aware electorate is more likely to price in the consequences of a conflict into subsequent elections. The more prepared the states are for an event, the less likely the event will be successful, and the less likely it will be attempted.

In an environment of debt defaults and government shutdowns, the most appropriate responses will come on the state level. If the states can organize an effective response to these threats, it will reduce the likelihood of an event. The higher the costs, the more likely the majority demographic group will retreat out of fear of economic loss or population loss. Democracies with state sovereignty and federalist systems have a better chance of imposing worse sanctions on majoritarian parties that may want to usurp power or secede.

There is another significant advantage to promoting a state-centric response. Their response will be more diverse there is a better chance to diffuse the situation or provoke a more moderate outcome. They can defer to the leadership of regional executives and rely on their ability to prepare emergency responses. The federal government may have more expertise and resources, but it may not be available after poor electoral outcomes for minority parties, or after debt defaults and prolonged government shutdowns. The states will have to determine their own security and chances for preserving both their voting rights and traditional territorial boundaries, which may be at risk.

Developing public policy and rhetoric is a huge advantage for those intending to preserve the union during a crisis. The opposition party can't openly dissent or prepare prior to the crises whereas loyalists can prepare contingency plans and openly advocate support for the nation. More importantly, they can expect their civil servants and public to support their policies. They can debate the benefits publicly and expect better electoral outcomes. If the culture can be changes prior to an event, the challenge can be avoided. Avoiding a conflict produces the best outcomes for the nation and its citizens.

The second biggest advantage is public finance. When there are imbalances in representation there are known weaknesses in public finance. In the United States, the Democratic states pay almost 57% of the taxes and only receive 50% of federalist tax dollars[66]. During an emergency, the Democratic states will have significant surpluses in revenues while the Republican States suffer large deficits. Reminding the opposition party of their dependence on federal tax subsidies will discourage many of their supporters and prevent them from acting on their threats of secession.

These arguments can be used prior to a dissolution or conflict to convince more red state governors or voters to preserve the union and refrain from debt defaults or government shutdowns. If the Republican States examine their finances prior to an event, provoked by Democratic state public policy and emergency preparation, many more will fear the shortfall in revenues and opt to stay in the Union. The Republican States only pay 43% of federal tax revenues but

---

[66] Table 8: Payments and Revenues 2015 (Democrats)

receive 50% of all federal subsidies, resulting in a loss of 20%, of revenues prior to assuming the liabilities of a dissolved federal military and other discretionary departments[67]. The shortfalls will need to be made up with taxes equivalent to twice that of current federal rates, before pricing in emergency police or armed forces costs. A dissolution or default will disrupt the market economy putting even downward pressure on tax revenues.

If undeterred, the Republicans are likely to successful secede regardless of which party is in office. Democrats have much more to lose from conflict than to gain from peaceful separation. A default will erode many of the advantages of peaceful dissolution without the antecedent of war necessarily occurring. This outcome results in the worst outcomes. It disrupts the Democrat's ability to discourage state-sanctioned violence with economic sanctions and trade treaties. Most of the repatriated dollars will be used to steady the consequences of default to the financial system.

Peaceful dissolution gives the Democratic states opportunity to leverage their massive economic advantage when Republican states are in state of emergency due to public finance crises. Democrats can use repatriated dollars to support aggressive immigration policies to relocate vulnerable populations from risky area of country to more secure and less populated regions within their territorial boundaries. Democrats can also use economic sanctions to coerce performance from Republican States to ensure former citizens are secure from loss of property or violence. The alternative to peaceful dissolution is economic ruin, resulting in permanent loss of GDP and tax revenue for all states.

The threat of demographic violence in the Republican states is high and there are no guarantees of protecting it, even with economic sanctions or a threat of military intervention. The Republican states will be suffering under public finance crises, with populations protesting and likely rioting. It won't take much for them to forcibly oppress minority populations and deploy force to validate their decisions. Republicans will be seeking to alter the demographics of voter dispositions so

---

[67] Table 9: Payments and Revenues 2015 (Republicans)

that they can maintain political dominance in a democracy. After the split, they will rely on incarceration or manslaughter to achieve these goals.

The Republicans are on the clock. Demographic-violence is often timed to occur just prior to the emergent demographic group gaining numerical superiority in late adolescent and young adult populations. War efforts require significant numbers of physically fit recruits, and demographic shifts result in a severe dilapidation in expectations for performance. For example, if half of all children in the nation are ethnicities other than the majority-demographic group, then despite maintaining a superior position in voters and wealth, they may have trouble recruiting an army from younger generations. This sunset clause creates urgency in the majority-demographic group evidenced by their irrational support for debt default threats and government shutdowns.

The threat pf authoritarianism can persist for years after the demographic-majority group becomes outnumbered by the new emergent demographic groups. Even a small number of ideologues supported by the aristocracy poses a risk. Most wars of rebellion or usurpation are fought by small margins of ideologues. A demographic group of 30-40% overall population will still occupy the highest echelons of the military, political offices, and industry. They could easily leverage and support a fighting force of just 1-2% of the total population.

The United States has already entered this phase of the demographic shift. This is the most dangerous period, where Caucasians are still more than 60% of the population, but represent less than 50% of all children[68], when threats of debt default are frequent, and government shutdowns have lasted for longer than 1 month[69]. The United States has the worst

---

[68] Jens Manuel Krogstad (July 31, 2019). "A view of the nation's future through kindergarten demographics". Retrieved from https://www.-pewresearch.org/fact-tank/2019/07/31/-kindergarten-demographics-in-us/?fbclid=IwAR2KUcxTv4aV7-EZH2kX-SpvEaiYmmGvCfEa-6TjdGwvqzaf4AFaqKqvHNhy4

[69] Mihir Zaveri, Guilbert Gates, and Karen Zraick (January 25 2019). "The Government Shutdown Was the Longest Ever. Here's the History", retrieved from https://www.nytimes.com/interactive/2019/01/09/us/politics/longest-government-shutdown.html

wealth inequality in 100 years[70] and an extremely low legislative production rate compared to prior years[71]. There are no examples of contemporary democracies successful navigating a demographic shift where one majority group peaceably transfers political power to a plurality of other ethnicities. If one looks at number of obstacles currently facing the United States, no one should be 100% certain that both voting rights and current territorial boundaries are preserved.

---

[70] Drew Desilver (December 5 2013). "U.S. income inequality, on rise for decades, is now highest since 1928", retrieved from
https://www.pewresearch.org/fact-tank/2013/12/05/u-s-income-inequality-on-rise-for-decades-is-now-highest-since-1928/
[71]" Statistics and Historical Comparison". Gov Track., retrieved on https://www.govtrack.us/congress/-bills/statistics

Bibliography

"America's Choice 2012 Election Center", Nov 2014, CNN
    Politics, retrieved from http://www.cnn.com/election/-
    201-2/results/-race/governor/

Chafetz, J. (2011). "The Unconstitutionality or the Filibuster".
    Connecticut Law Review, Vol 43, No. 4, pp. 1003-1040,
    May 2011. retrieved from https://papers.-ssrn.com/sol3/-
    papers.-cfm?abstract_id=1730782

"Democracy Index 2018: Me too?", 2019, The Economist
    Intelligence Unit, www.eiu.com

Department of Treasury, "Internal Revenue Service Data
    Book 2017", retrieved from https://-www.irs.-gov/pub/-
    irssoi/17-databk.pdf

Desilver, Drew (December 5 2013). "U.S. income inequality,
    on rise for decades, is now highest since 1928".
    Retrieved from https://www.pewresearch.org/fact-
    tank/2013/12/05/u-s-income-inequality-on-rise-for-
    decades-is-now-highest-since-1928/

Eichler, Alexander & McAuliff, Michael, "Income Inequality
    Reached Gilded Age Levels, Congressional Report
    Finds", last updated Dec 6th 2017, Huffpost, retrieved
    from https://ww-w.huffpost-.com/entry/income-inequal-
    ity_n_10326

"Election 2016", Nov 2016, CNN Politics, retrieved from
    https://www.-cnn.com/-

"GDP Growth (Annual %)", World Bank, Retrieved from
    https://data.worldbank.org/indicator/NY.GDP.MKTP.K
    D.ZG?locations=US

Gill, N.S., "The Roman Republics Government", March 30th,
    2019, retrieved from https://www.th-oughtco.com/the-
    roman-   republics-government-120772

"GINI Index (World Bank Estimate)". World Bank, retrieved
from https://data.worldbank.org/-indicator/SI.POV.GINI

Gruber, Jonathan (2013), "Public Finance and Public Policy",
4ed, Worth Publishers, New York, NY.

Kong, Cameron, "Recession is Overdue by 4.5 Years. Here is
How to Prepare". Forbes.com, Oct 23, 2018, retrieved
from https://www.forbes.com/sites/cameronkeng/-2018-
/10/23/-recessionis-overdue-by-4-5-years-heres-how-to-
prepare/#5710753240d8

Krogstad, Jens Manuel, (07/31/2019) "A view of the nation's
future through kindergarten", retried from
https://www.pewresearch.-org/fact-tank/2019/07/31-
/kindergarten-demographics-in-us/?fbclid=IwAR2K-
UcxTv4a-V7EZH2kX-SpvEaiYmmGvCfEa6T-
jdGwvqzaf4AFaq-KqvHNhy4

Legion, Thomas. "Population of the Original 13 Colonies",
retrieved From http://-www.thomas-legion.net/-
population_of_the_orig-inal_thirteen_colonies_-
free_slave_white_and_nonwhite.html

Longley, Robert, "Direct Democracy Pros and Cons", July 7th,
2019, retrieved from https://www.th-oughtco.com/what-
is-direct-democracy- 3322038

Murse, Tom. Aug 30 2019, "Why the Presidents Party Loses
Seats in The Midterm Elections", retrieved from https-
://www.thoughtco.-com/historical-midterm-election-
results-4087704

Przeworski, Adam. "Minimalist Conception of Democracy: A
Defense" Democracy's Value, edited by Shapiro, I. and
Hacker-Cordon, C. (Cambridge: Cambridge University
Press, 1999

Politico, "Election Central", updated 12/23/2014, retrieved

from https-://www.politico.c-om/2014-election/-results/map/-governor#-.XSyJkPZFz85

"Statistics and Historical Comparison". Gov Track. Retrieved on https://www.govtrack.us/congress/bills/statistics

Stone, Lyman, 9/24/2014 "Which States have the most progressive income taxes", retrieved from https://taxfoundation.org/which-states-have-most-progressive-income-taxes-0/

Woods, Darian, 06/25/2019 "The Magic Number Behind Protests", accessed on 9/10/2019, retrieved from https://www.npr.org/ sections/money/2019/06/25/7-35536434/ the-magic-number-behind-protests

Zaveri, M., Gates, G., and Zraick, K. (January 25 2019). "The Government Shutdown Was the Longest Ever. Here's the History", retrieved from https://www.nytimes.com/-interactive/2019/01/09/us/politics/longest-government-shutdown.html

"2018 National and State Population Estimates", U.S. Census, accessed on 7/9/2019, retrieved from https://www.census-s.gov/newsroom/press-kits/2018/pop-estimates-national-state.html

Table 1: Tax-based Coefficients (Democrats)[72]

State	Revenues (in millions)	# Reps Revenue in Union	%	# Reps Revenue Split	%	Party
Vermont	$4,495.28	1	0.14%	1	0.24%	Democrat
Maine	$7,464.28	1	0.23%	2	0.41%	Democrat
Hawaii	$8,221.29	1	0.25%	2	0.45%	Democrat
New Mexico	$8,969.67	1	0.28%	2	0.49%	Democrat
New Hampshire	$11,314.99	2	0.35%	3	0.62%	Democrat
Rhode Island	$14,373.32	2	0.44%	3	0.78%	Democrat
Nevada	$18,450.07	2	0.57%	4	1.00%	Democrat
Delaware	$22,640.85	3	0.70%	5	1.23%	Democrat
Oregon	$31,219.15	4	0.96%	7	1.70%	Democrat
Colorado	$47,210.72	6	1.45%	11	2.57%	Democrat
Wisconsin	$51,748.83	7	1.59%	12	2.81%	Democrat
Connecticut	$59,174.58	8	1.82%	14	3.22%	Democrat
Maryland	$63,936.80	9	1.97%	15	3.48%	Democrat
Washington	$73,334.44	10	2.25%	17	3.99%	Democrat
Michigan	$77,948.41	10	2.40%	18	4.24%	Democrat
Minnesota	$106,927.81	14	3.29%	25	5.81%	Democrat
Massachusetts	$108,049.21	14	3.32%	26	5.88%	Democrat
Pennsylvania	$136,108.81	18	4.18%	32	7.40%	Democrat
New Jersey	$153,917.57	21	4.73%	36	8.37%	Democrat
Illinois	$158,042.27	21	4.86%	37	8.59%	Democrat
New York	$269,717.00	36	8.29%	64	14.67%	Democrat
California	$405,851.30	54	12.48%	96	22.07%	Democrat
Total	$1,839,116.64	246	56.54%	435	100.00%	
Divisor	$4,227.85					

[72] Table created from Department of Treasury, Internal Revenue Service Data Book 2017, Accessed 7/8/2019, Retrieved from https://-www.irs.gov/pub/irs-soi/17databk.pdf

Table 2: Tax-based Coefficients (Republicans)[73]

State	Revenues (in millions)	# Reps Revenue in Union	%	# Reps Revenue Split	%	Party
Wyoming	$5,284.15	1	0.16%	2	0.37%	Republican
Alaska	$5,717.64	1	0.18%	2	0.40%	Republican
Montana	$5,805.10	1	0.18%	2	0.41%	Republican
West Virginia	$7,374.30	1	0.23%	2	0.52%	Republican
North Dakota	$7,711.24	1	0.24%	2	0.55%	Republican
South Dakota	$7,732.14	1	0.24%	2	0.55%	Republican
Idaho	$9,785.03	1	0.30%	3	0.69%	Republican
Mississippi	$11,468.66	2	0.35%	4	0.81%	Republican
Utah	$20,178.72	3	0.62%	6	1.43%	Republican
Iowa	$23,969.39	3	0.74%	7	1.70%	Republican
South Carolina	$24,086.26	3	0.74%	7	1.70%	Republican
Alabama	$25,070.26	3	0.77%	8	1.77%	Republican
Nebraska	$25,103.77	3	0.77%	8	1.78%	Republican
Kansas	$27,019.29	4	0.83%	8	1.91%	Republican
Arkansas	$32,508.76	4	1.00%	10	2.30%	Republican
Kentucky	$32,708.39	4	1.00%	10	2.31%	Republican
Oklahoma	$33,942.29	5	1.04%	10	2.40%	Republican
Louisiana	$42,628.15	6	1.31%	13	3.01%	Republican
Arizona	$42,631.32	6	1.31%	13	3.02%	Republican
Indiana	$57,972.83	8	1.78%	18	4.10%	Republican
Tennessee	$62,708.66	8	1.92%	19	4.44%	Republican
Missouri	$64,112.50	9	1.97%	20	4.53%	Republican
North Carolina	$78,736.40	11	2.42%	24	5.57%	Republican
Virginia	$80,242.85	11	2.46%	25	5.68%	Republican
Georgia	$86,446.60	12	2.65%	27	6.11%	Republican
Ohio	$140,981.15	19	4.33%	43	9.97%	Republican
Florida	$177,389.49	24	5.44%	55	12.55%	Republican
Texas	$279,904.43	37	8.59%	86	19.80%	Republican
Total	$1,413,935.61	189	43.56%	435	100%	
Divisor	$3,250.43					
Union	$3,253,052	435				
Union Divisor	$7,478.28					

[73] Table created from Department of Treasury, Internal Revenue Service Data Book 2017, Accessed 7/8/2019, Retrieved from https://-www.irs.gov/pub/irs-soi/17databk.pdf

Table 3: Above Median Chamber (by Population)[74]

State	Population	Revenues (in millions)	# Reps population	%	Median Partition by Revenue	Party
Massachusetts	6,784,240	$108,049.21	9	4.24%	Upper	Democrat
Pennsylvania	12,791,904	$136,108.81	17	7.99%	Upper	Democrat
New Jersey	8,935,421	$153,917.57	12	5.58%	Upper	Democrat
Illinois	12,839,047	$158,042.27	17	8.02%	Upper	Democrat
New York	19,747,183	$269,717.00	27	12.33%	Upper	Democrat
California	38,993,940	$405,851.30	53	24.35%	Upper	Democrat
Minnesota			1	0.46%	Upper	Democrat
Ohio	11,605,090	$140,981.15	16	7.25%	Upper	Republican
Florida	20,244,914	$177,389.49	27	12.64%	Upper	Republican
Texas	27,429,639	$279,904.43	37	17.13%	Upper	Republican
Total # of Seats			217			All
Total # of Seats			137	62.98%		Democrat
Total # of Seats			80	37.02%		Republican
Totals	320,226,241	$1,419,219.75				
Union Totals	320,226,241	$1,419,220				
Union Divisors	737848.482	$3,270.09				

[74] Table created from U.S. Census, 2018 National and State Population Estimates, accessed on 7/9/2019, retrieved from https://www.censu-s.gov/newsroom/press-kits/2018/pop-estimates-national-state.html and Department of Treasury, Internal Revenue Service Data Book 2017, Accessed 7/8/2019, Retrieved from https://-www.irs.gov/pub/irs-soi/17databk.pdf

Table 4: Below Median Chamber (Democratic, by Population)[75]

State	Population	Revenues (in millions)	# Reps population	%	Median Partition by Revenue	Party
Vermont	626,088	$4,495.28	1	0.39%	Lower	Democrat
Maine	1,329,453	$7,464.28	2	0.83%	Lower	Democrat
Hawaii	1,425,157	$8,221.29	2	0.89%	Lower	Democrat
New Mexico	2,080,328	$8,969.67	3	1.30%	Lower	Democrat
New Hampshire	1,330,111	$11,314.99	2	0.83%	Lower	Democrat
Rhode Island	1,055,607	$14,373.32	1	0.66%	Lower	Democrat
Nevada	2,883,758	$18,450.07	4	1.80%	Lower	Democrat
Delaware	944,076	$22,640.85	1	0.59%	Lower	Democrat
Oregon	4,024,634	$31,219.15	5	2.51%	Lower	Democrat
Colorado	5,448,819	$47,210.72	7	3.40%	Lower	Democrat
Wisconsin	5,767,891	$51,748.83	8	3.60%	Lower	Democrat
Connecticut	3,584,730	$59,174.58	5	2.24%	Lower	Democrat
Maryland	5,994,983	$63,936.80	8	3.74%	Lower	Democrat
Washington	7,160,290	$73,334.44	10	4.47%	Lower	Democrat
Michigan	9,917,715	$77,948.41	13	6.19%	Lower	Democrat
Minnesota	5,482,435	$106,927.81	6	2.76%	Lower	Democrat

---

[75] Table created from U.S. Census, 2018 National and State Population Estimates, accessed on 7/9/2019, retrieved from https://www.censu-s.gov/newsroom/press-kits/2018/pop-estimates-national-state.html and Department of Treasury, Internal Revenue Service Data Book 2017, Accessed 7/8/2019, Retrieved from https://-www.irs.gov/pub/irs-soi/17databk.pdf

Table 5: Below Median Chamber (Republican, by Population)[76]

State	Population	Revenues (in millions)	# Reps population	%	Median Partition by Revenue	Party
Wyoming	586,555	$5,284.15	1	0.37%	Lower	Republican
Alaska	737,709	$5,717.64	1	0.46%	Lower	Republican
Montana	1,032,073	$5,805.10	1	0.64%	Lower	Republican
West Virginia	1,841,053	$7,374.30	2	1.15%	Lower	Republican
North Dakota	756,835	$7,711.24	1	0.47%	Lower	Republican
South Dakota	857,919	$7,732.14	1	0.54%	Lower	Republican
Idaho	1,652,828	$9,785.03	2	1.03%	Lower	Republican
Mississippi	2,989,390	$11,468.66	4	1.87%	Lower	Republican
Utah	2,990,632	$20,178.72	4	1.87%	Lower	Republican
Iowa	3,121,997	$23,969.39	4	1.95%	Lower	Republican
South Carolina	4,894,834	$24,086.26	7	3.06%	Lower	Republican
Alabama	4,853,875	$25,070.26	7	3.03%	Lower	Republican
Nebraska	1,893,765	$25,103.77	3	1.18%	Lower	Republican
Kansas	2,906,721	$27,019.29	4	1.82%	Lower	Republican
Arkansas	2,977,853	$32,508.76	4	1.86%	Lower	Republican
Kentucky	4,424,611	$32,708.39	6	2.76%	Lower	Republican
Oklahoma	3,907,414	$33,942.29	5	2.44%	Lower	Republican
Louisiana	4,668,960	$42,628.15	6	2.92%	Lower	Republican
Arizona	6,817,565	$42,631.32	9	4.26%	Lower	Republican
Indiana	6,612,768	$57,972.83	9	4.13%	Lower	Republican
Tennessee	6,595,056	$62,708.66	9	4.12%	Lower	Republican
Missouri	6,076,204	$64,112.50	8	3.79%	Lower	Republican
North Carolina	10,035,186	$78,736.40	14	6.27%	Lower	Republican
Virginia	8,367,587	$80,242.85	11	5.23%	Lower	Republican
Georgia	10,199,398	$86,446.60	14	6.37%	Lower	Republican
Total # of Seats			217			
Total # of Seats			79	36.30%		Democrat
Total # of Seats			138	63.70%		Republican

[76] Table created from U.S. Census, 2018 National and State Population Estimates, accessed on 7/9/2019, retrieved from https://www.censu-s.gov/newsroom/press-kits/2018/pop-estimates-national-state.html and Department of Treasury, Internal Revenue Service Data Book 2017, Accessed 7/8/2019, Retrieved from https://-www.irs.gov/pub/irs-soi/17databk.pdf

Table 6: Per Capita Tax Liabilities (Democratic)[77]

State	Population	Average Tax liability (Per capita)	# Reps - Partisan	%	# of Reps - Full	%	Partisanship
Vermont	626,088	$7,179.95	13	2.92%	7	1.51%	Democrat
Maine	1,329,453	$5,614.55	10	2.28%	5	1.18%	Democrat
Hawaii	1,425,157	$5,768.69	10	2.35%	5	1.21%	Democrat
New Mexico	2,080,328	$4,311.66	8	1.75%	4	0.91%	Democrat
New Hampshire	1,330,111	$8,506.80	15	3.46%	8	1.79%	Democrat
Rhode Island	1,055,607	$13,616.16	24	5.54%	12	2.86%	Democrat
Nevada	2,883,758	$6,397.93	11	2.60%	6	1.34%	Democrat
Delaware	944,076	$23,982.02	42	9.76%	22	5.03%	Democrat
Oregon	4,024,634	$7,757.02	14	3.16%	7	1.63%	Democrat
Colorado	5,448,819	$8,664.39	15	3.53%	8	1.82%	Democrat
Wisconsin	5,767,891	$8,971.88	16	3.65%	8	1.88%	Democrat
Connecticut	3,584,730	$16,507.40	29	6.72%	15	3.47%	Democrat
Maryland	5,994,983	$10,665.05	19	4.34%	10	2.24%	Democrat
Washington	7,160,290	$10,241.82	18	4.17%	9	2.15%	Democrat
Michigan	9,917,715	$7,859.51	14	3.20%	7	1.65%	Democrat
Minnesota	5,482,435	$19,503.71	35	7.94%	18	4.09%	Democrat
Massachusetts	6,784,240	$15,926.50	28	6.48%	15	3.34%	Democrat
Pennsylvania	12,791,904	$10,640.23	19	4.33%	10	2.23%	Democrat
New Jersey	8,935,421	$17,225.55	30	7.01%	16	3.62%	Democrat
Illinois	12,839,047	$12,309.50	22	5.01%	11	2.58%	Democrat
New York	19,747,183	$13,658.51	24	5.56%	12	2.87%	Democrat
California	38,993,940	$10,408.06	18	4.24%	10	2.18%	Democrat
Total	159,147,810	$11,168.95	435	100.00%	224	51.58%	Democrat
Divisor		564.87					

[77] Table created from U.S. Census, 2018 National and State Population Estimates, accessed on 7/9/2019, retrieved from https://www.census.gov/newsroom/press-kits/2018/pop-estimates-national-state.html and Department of Treasury, Internal Revenue Service Data Book 2017, Accessed 7/8/2019, Retrieved from https://-www.irs.gov/pub/irs-soi/17databk.pdf

Table 7: Per Capita Tax Liabilities (Republican)[78]

State	Population	Average Tax liability (Per capita)	# Reps - Partisan		# of Reps - Full		Partisanship
Virginia	8,367,587	$9,589.72	18	4.16%	9	2.01%	Republican
Alabama	4,853,875	$5,165.00	10	2.24%	5	1.08%	Republican
South Carolina	4,894,834	$4,920.75	9	2.13%	4	1.03%	Republican
Arizona	6,817,565	$6,253.16	12	2.71%	6	1.31%	Republican
Mississippi	2,989,390	$3,836.45	7	1.66%	4	0.81%	Republican
Kentucky	4,424,611	$7,392.38	14	3.21%	7	1.55%	Republican
North Carolina	10,035,186	$7,846.03	15	3.40%	7	1.65%	Republican
West Virginia	1,841,053	$4,005.48	8	1.74%	4	0.84%	Republican
Florida	20,244,914	$8,762.18	17	3.80%	8	1.84%	Republican
Idaho	1,652,828	$5,920.17	11	2.57%	5	1.24%	Republican
Alaska	737,709	$7,750.54	15	3.36%	7	1.63%	Republican
Montana	1,032,073	$5,624.70	11	2.44%	5	1.18%	Republican
Oklahoma	3,907,414	$8,686.64	16	3.77%	8	1.82%	Republican
Georgia	10,199,398	$8,475.66	16	3.67%	8	1.78%	Republican
Louisiana	4,668,960	$9,130.12	17	3.96%	8	1.92%	Republican
Iowa	3,121,997	$7,677.58	14	3.33%	7	1.61%	Republican
Tennessee	6,595,056	$9,508.44	18	4.12%	9	2.00%	Republican
Missouri	6,076,204	$10,551.41	20	4.57%	10	2.22%	Republican
Utah	2,990,632	$6,747.31	13	2.93%	6	1.42%	Republican
South Dakota	857,919	$9,012.67	17	3.91%	8	1.89%	Republican
Wyoming	586,555	$9,008.78	17	3.91%	8	1.89%	Republican
North Dakota	756,835	$10,188.80	19	4.42%	9	2.14%	Republican
Indiana	6,612,768	$8,766.80	17	3.80%	8	1.84%	Republican
Kansas	2,906,721	$9,295.45	18	4.03%	8	1.95%	Republican
Arkansas	2,977,853	$10,916.85	21	4.73%	10	2.29%	Republican
Nebraska	1,893,765	$13,256.01	25	5.75%	12	2.78%	Republican
Ohio	11,605,090	$12,148.22	23	5.27%	11	2.55%	Republican
Texas	27,429,639	$10,204.45	19	4.42%	9	2.14%	Republican
Total	161,078,431	$8,237.20	435	100.00%	211	48.42%	Republican
Union Total	320,226,241	530			1095.07733		
Union Divisor	736152.278						

---

[78] Table created from U.S. Census, 2018 National and State Population Estimates, accessed on 7/9/2019, retrieved from https://www.censu-s.gov/newsroom/press-kits/2018/pop-estimates-national-state.html and Department of Treasury, Internal Revenue Service Data Book 2017, Accessed 7/8/2019, Retrieved from https://-www.irs.gov/pub/irs-soi/17databk.pdf

Table 8: Table of Payments and Revenues 2017 (Democrats)[79]

State	Population	Total Subsidies (in millions)	Revenues (in millions)	Rev - Spending (in millions)	Average Tax liability (Per capita)	Partisanship
Maryland	5,994,983	$92,987	$63,936.80	$ (29,050.20)	$10,665.05	Democrat
New Mexico	2,080,328	$27,554	$8,969.67	$ (18,584.33)	$4,311.66	Democrat
Michigan	9,917,715	$94,014	$77,948.41	$ (16,065.59)	$7,859.51	Democrat
Hawaii	1,425,157	$19,309	$8,221.29	$ (11,087.71)	$5,768.69	Democrat
Maine	1,329,453	$16,078	$7,464.28	$ (8,613.72)	$5,614.55	Democrat
Nevada	2,883,758	$23,181	$18,450.07	$ (4,730.93)	$6,397.93	Democrat
Vermont	626,088	$6,915	$4,495.28	$ (2,419.72)	$7,179.95	Democrat
Oregon	4,024,634	$32,713	$31,219.15	$ (1,493.85)	$7,757.02	Democrat
Colorado	5,448,819	$48,664	$47,210.72	$ (1,453.28)	$8,664.39	Democrat
New Hampshire	1,330,111	$12,414	$11,314.99	$ (1,099.02)	$8,506.80	Democrat
Washington	7,160,290	$72,937	$73,334.44	$ 397.44	$10,241.82	Democrat
Pennsylvania	12,791,904	$134,989	$136,108.81	$ 1,119.81	$10,640.23	Democrat
Rhode Island	1,055,607	$11,549	$14,373.32	$ 2,824.32	$13,616.16	Democrat
Wisconsin	5,767,891	$47,735	$51,748.83	$ 4,013.83	$8,971.88	Democrat
Delaware	944,076	$9,047	$22,640.85	$ 13,593.85	$23,982.02	Democrat
Connecticut	3,584,730	$41,452	$59,174.58	$ 17,722.58	$16,507.40	Democrat
Massachusetts	6,784,240	$75,631	$108,049.21	$ 32,418.21	$15,926.50	Democrat
Illinois	12,839,047	$105,483	$158,042.27	$ 52,559.27	$12,309.50	Democrat
California	38,993,940	$343,725	$405,851.30	$ 62,126.30	$10,408.06	Democrat
Minnesota	5,482,435	$44,304	$106,927.81	$ 62,623.81	$19,503.71	Democrat
New Jersey	8,935,421	$82,573	$153,917.57	$ 71,344.57	$17,225.55	Democrat
New York	19,747,183	$195,334	$269,717.00	$ 74,383.00	$13,658.51	Democrat
Totals	159,147,810	$1,538,588	$1,839,116.64	$ 300,528.64	$11,168.95	

[79] Table created from Department of Treasury, Internal Revenue Service Data Book 2017, Accessed 7/8/2019, Retrieved from https://-www.irs.gov/pub/irs-soi/17databk.pdf

Table 9: Payments and Revenues 2017 (Republicans)[80]

State	Population	Total Subsidies (in millions)	Revenues (in millions)	Rev - Spending (in millions)	Average Tax liability (Per capita)	Partisanship
Virginia	8,367,587	$138,029	$80,242.85	$ (57,786.15)	$9,589.72	Republican
Alabama	4,853,875	$56,762	$25,070.26	$ (31,691.74)	$5,165.00	Republican
South Carolina	4,894,834	$48,784	$24,086.26	$ (24,697.74)	$4,920.75	Republican
Arizona	6,817,565	$67,306	$42,631.32	$ (24,674.68)	$6,253.16	Republican
Mississippi	2,989,390	$34,308	$11,468.66	$ (22,839.34)	$3,836.45	Republican
Kentucky	4,424,611	$48,027	$32,708.39	$ (15,318.61)	$7,392.38	Republican
North Carolina	10,035,186	$93,907	$78,736.40	$ (15,170.60)	$7,846.03	Republican
West Virginia	1,841,053	$21,317	$7,374.30	$ (13,942.70)	$4,005.48	Republican
Florida	20,244,914	$190,831	$177,389.49	$ (13,441.51)	$8,762.18	Republican
Idaho	1,652,828	$15,139	$9,785.03	$ (5,353.97)	$5,920.17	Republican
Alaska	737,709	$10,568	$5,717.64	$ (4,850.36)	$7,750.54	Republican
Montana	1,032,073	$10,148	$5,805.10	$ (4,342.90)	$5,624.70	Republican
Oklahoma	3,907,414	$37,851	$33,942.29	$ (3,908.71)	$8,686.64	Republican
Georgia	10,199,398	$88,532	$86,446.60	$ (2,085.40)	$8,475.66	Republican
Louisiana	4,668,960	$44,701	$42,628.15	$ (2,072.85)	$9,130.12	Republican
Iowa	3,121,997	$25,883	$23,969.39	$ (1,913.61)	$7,677.58	Republican
Tennessee	6,595,056	$64,508	$62,708.66	$ (1,799.34)	$9,508.44	Republican
Missouri	6,076,204	$65,452	$64,112.50	$ (1,339.50)	$10,551.41	Republican
Utah	2,990,632	$20,620	$20,178.72	$ (441.28)	$6,747.31	Republican
South Dakota	857,919	$8,025	$7,732.14	$ (292.86)	$9,012.67	Republican
Wyoming	586,555	$5,177	$5,284.15	$ 107.15	$9,008.78	Republican
North Dakota	756,835	$6,805	$7,711.24	$ 906.24	$10,188.80	Republican
Indiana	6,612,768	$55,496	$57,972.83	$ 2,476.83	$8,766.80	Republican
Kansas	2,906,721	$24,243	$27,019.29	$ 2,776.29	$9,295.45	Republican
Arkansas	2,977,853	$28,514	$32,508.76	$ 3,994.76	$10,916.85	Republican
Nebraska	1,893,765	$15,636	$25,103.77	$ 9,467.77	$13,256.01	Republican
Ohio	11,605,090	$101,573	$140,981.15	$ 39,408.15	$12,148.22	Republican
Texas	27,429,639	$234,459	$279,904.43	$ 45,445.43	$10,204.45	Republican
Totals	161,078,431	$1,562,601	$1,419,219.75	$ (143,381.25)	$8,237.20	

[80] Table created from Department of Treasury, Internal Revenue Service Data Book 2017, Accessed 7/8/2019, Retrieved from https://-www.irs.gov/pub/irs-soi/17databk.pdf

Table 10: Net Chamber Eligibility (Democrats)[81]

State	Population	Total Subsidies (in millions)	Revenues (in millions)	Rev - Spending (in millions)	Average Tax liability (Per capita)	Partisanship
California	38,993,940	$343,725	$405,851.30	$ 62,126.30	$10,408.06	Democrat
Colorado	5,448,819	$48,664	$47,210.72	$ (1,453.28)	$8,664.39	Democrat
Connecticut	3,584,730	$41,452	$59,174.58	$ 17,722.58	$16,507.40	Democrat
Delaware	944,076	$9,047	$22,640.85	$ 13,593.85	$23,982.02	Democrat
Hawaii	1,425,157	$19,309	$8,221.29	$ (11,087.71)	$5,768.69	Democrat
Illinois	12,839,047	$105,483	$158,042.27	$ 52,559.27	$12,309.50	Democrat
Maine	1,329,453	$16,078	$7,464.28	$ (8,613.72)	$5,614.55	Democrat
Maryland	5,994,983	$92,987	$63,936.80	$ (29,050.20)	$10,665.05	Democrat
Massachusetts	6,784,240	$75,631	$108,049.21	$ 32,418.21	$15,926.50	Democrat
Michigan	9,917,715	$94,014	$77,948.41	$ (16,065.59)	$7,859.51	Democrat
Minnesota	5,482,435	$44,304	$106,927.81	$ 62,623.81	$19,503.71	Democrat
Nevada	2,883,758	$23,181	$18,450.07	$ (4,730.93)	$6,397.93	Democrat
New Hampshire	1,330,111	$12,414	$11,314.99	$ (1,099.02)	$8,506.80	Democrat
New Jersey	8,935,421	$82,573	$153,917.57	$ 71,344.57	$17,225.55	Democrat
New Mexico	2,080,328	$27,554	$8,969.67	$ (18,584.33)	$4,311.66	Democrat
New York	19,747,183	$195,334	$269,717.00	$ 74,383.00	$13,658.51	Democrat
Oregon	4,024,634	$32,713	$31,219.15	$ (1,493.85)	$7,757.02	Democrat
Pennsylvania	12,791,904	$134,989	$136,108.81	$ 1,119.81	$10,640.23	Democrat
Rhode Island	1,055,607	$11,549	$14,373.32	$ 2,824.32	$13,616.16	Democrat
Vermont	626,088	$6,915	$4,495.28	$ (2,419.72)	$7,179.95	Democrat
Washington	7,160,290	$72,937	$73,334.44	$ 397.44	$10,241.82	Democrat
Wisconsin	5,767,891	$47,735	$51,748.83	$ 4,013.83	$8,971.88	Democrat
Totals	159,147,810	$1,538,588	$1,839,116.64	$ 300,528.64	$11,168.95	

---

[81] Table created from U.S. Census, 2018 National and State Population Estimates, accessed on 7/9/2019, retrieved from https://www.censu-s.gov/newsroom/press-kits/2018/pop-estimates-national-state.html and Department of Treasury, Internal Revenue Service Data Book 2017, Accessed 7/8/2019, Retrieved from https://-www.irs.gov/pub/irs-soi/17databk.pdf

Table 11: Net Chamber Eligibility (Republicans)[82]

State	Population	Rev - Spending	Party	Net Chamber	# of Reps Net Population	%	# of Reps Net Revenues	%
Virginia	8,367,587	$ (57,786.15)	Republican	Ineligible				
Alabama	4,853,875	$ (31,691.74)	Republican	Ineligible				
South Carolina	4,894,834	$ (24,697.74)	Republican	Ineligible				
Arizona	6,817,565	$ (24,674.68)	Republican	Ineligible				
Mississippi	2,989,390	$ (22,839.34)	Republican	Ineligible				
Kentucky	4,424,611	$ (15,318.61)	Republican	Ineligible				
North Carolina	10,035,186	$ (15,170.60)	Republican	Ineligible				
West Virginia	1,841,053	$ (13,942.70)	Republican	Ineligible				
Florida	20,244,914	$ (13,441.51)	Republican	Ineligible				
Idaho	1,652,828	$ (5,353.97)	Republican	Ineligible				
Alaska	737,709	$ (4,850.36)	Republican	Ineligible				
Montana	1,032,073	$ (4,342.90)	Republican	Ineligible				
Oklahoma	3,907,414	$ (3,908.71)	Republican	Ineligible				
Georgia	10,199,398	$ (2,085.40)	Republican	Ineligible				
Louisiana	4,668,960	$ (2,072.85)	Republican	Ineligible				
Iowa	3,121,997	$ (1,913.61)	Republican	Ineligible				
Tennessee	6,595,056	$ (1,799.34)	Republican	Ineligible				
Missouri	6,076,204	$ (1,339.50)	Republican	Ineligible				
Utah	2,990,632	$ (441.28)	Republican	Ineligible				
South Dakota	857,919	$ (292.86)	Republican	Ineligible				
Wyoming	586,555	$ 107.15	Republican	Net Eligible	1	0.33%	0	0.02%
North Dakota	756,835	$ 906.24	Republican	Net Eligible	2	0.42%	1	0.18%
Indiana	6,612,768	$ 2,476.83	Republican	Net Eligible	16	3.70%	2	0.50%
Kansas	2,906,721	$ 2,776.29	Republican	Net Eligible	7	1.63%	2	0.56%
Arkansas	2,977,853	$ 3,994.76	Republican	Net Eligible	7	1.66%	3	0.80%
Nebraska	1,893,765	$ 9,467.77	Republican	Net Eligible	5	1.06%	8	1.89%
Ohio	11,605,090	$ 39,408.15	Republican	Net Eligible	28	6.49%	34	7.89%
Texas	27,429,639	$ 45,445.43	Republican	Net Eligible	67	15.34%	40	9.09%
Totals	161,078,431	$ (143,381.25)		8	133	30.62%	91	20.93%

---

[82] Table created from U.S. Census, 2018 National and State Population Estimates, accessed on 7/9/2019, retrieved from https://www.censu-s.gov/newsroom/press-kits/2018/pop-estimates-national-state.html and Department of Treasury, Internal Revenue Service Data Book 2017, Accessed 7/8/2019, Retrieved from https://-www.irs.gov/pub/irs-soi/17databk.pdf

Made in the USA
Monee, IL
21 February 2020